MASTER THE™ DSST®

Criminal Justice Exam

About Peterson's

Peterson's® has been your trusted educational publisher for over 50 years. It's a milestone we're quite proud of, as we continue to offer the most accurate, dependable, high-quality educational content in the field, providing you with everything you need to succeed. No matter where you are on your academic or professional path, you can rely on Peterson's for its books, online information, expert test-prep tools, the most up-to-date education exploration data, and the highest quality career success resources—everything you need to achieve your education goals. For our complete line of products, visit www.petersons.com.

For more information, contact Peterson's, 8740 Lucent Blvd., Suite 400, Highlands Ranch, CO 80129; 800-338-3282 Ext. 54229; or find us online at **www.petersons.com**.

ISBN: 978-0-7689-4443-3

Printed in the United States of America

10 9 8 7 6 5 4 3 2 1   22 21 20

Contents

Before You Begin

HOW THIS BOOK IS ORGANIZED

Peterson's *Master the*™ *DSST® Criminal Justice Exam* provides a diagnostic test, subject-matter review, and a post-test.

- **Diagnostic Test**—Twenty multiple-choice questions, followed by an answer key with detailed answer explanations
- **Assessment Grid**—A chart designed to help you identify areas that you need to focus on based on your test results
- **Subject-Matter Review**—General overview of the exam subject, followed by a review of the relevant topics and terminology covered on the exam
- **Post-test**—Sixty multiple-choice questions, followed by an answer key and detailed answer explanations

The purpose of the diagnostic test is to help you figure out what you know—or don't know. The twenty multiple-choice questions are similar to the ones found on the DSST exam, and they should provide you with a good idea of what to expect. Once you take the diagnostic test, check your answers to see how you did. Included with each correct answer is a brief explanation regarding why a specific answer is correct, and in many cases, why other options are incorrect. Use the assessment grid to identify the questions you miss so that you can spend more time reviewing that information later. As with any exam, knowing your weak spots greatly improves your chances of success.

Following the diagnostic test is a subject-matter review. The review summarizes the various topics covered on the DSST exam. Key terms are defined; important concepts are explained; and when appropriate, examples are provided. As you read the review, some of the information may seem familiar while other information may seem foreign. Again, take note of the unfamiliar because that will most likely cause you problems on the actual exam.

After studying the subject-matter review, you should be ready for the post-test. The post-test contains sixty multiple-choice items, and it will serve as a dry run for the real DSST exam. There are complete answer explanations at the end of the test.

OTHER DSST® PRODUCTS BY PETERSON'S

Books, flashcards, practice tests, and videos available online at **www.petersons.com/testprep/dsst**

- Art of the Western World
- Astronomy
- Business Mathematics
- Business Ethics and Society
- Civil War and Reconstruction
- Computing and Information Technology
- Criminal Justice
- Environmental Science
- Ethics in America
- Ethics in Technology
- Foundations of Education
- Fundamentals of College Algebra
- Fundamentals of Counseling
- Fundamentals of Cybersecurity
- General Anthropology
- Health and Human Development
- History of the Soviet Union
- History of the Vietnam War
- Human Resource Management
- Introduction to Business
- Introduction to Geography
- Introduction to Geology
- Introduction to Law Enforcement
- Introduction to World Religions
- Lifespan Developmental Psychology
- Math for Liberal Arts
- Management Information Systems
- Money and Banking
- Organizational Behavior
- Personal Finance
- Principles of Advanced English Composition
- Principles of Finance
- Principles of Public Speaking
- Principles of Statistics
- Principles of Supervision
- Substance Abuse
- Technical Writing

Like what you see? Get unlimited access to Peterson's full catalog of DSST practice tests, instructional videos, flashcards and more for **75% off the first month!** Go to **www.petersons.com/testprep/dsst** and use coupon code **DSST2020** at checkout. Offer expires July 1, 2021.

Chapter 1

All About the DSST® Exam

WHAT IS DSST®?

Previously known as the DANTES Subject Standardized Tests, the DSST program provides the opportunity for individuals to earn college credit for what they have learned outside of the traditional classroom. Accepted or administered at more than 1,900 colleges and universities nationwide and approved by the American Council on Education (ACE), the DSST program enables individuals to use the knowledge they have acquired outside the classroom to accomplish their educational and professional goals.

WHY TAKE A DSST® EXAM?

DSST exams offer a way for you to save both time and money in your quest for a college education. Why enroll in a college course in a subject you already understand? For over 30 years, the DSST program has offered the perfect solution for individuals who are knowledgeable in a specific subject and want to save both time and money. A passing score on a DSST exam provides physical evidence to universities of proficiency in a specific subject. More than 1,900 accredited and respected colleges and universities across the nation award undergraduate credit for passing scores on DSST exams. With the DSST program, individuals can shave months off the time it takes to earn a degree.

The DSST program offers numerous advantages for individuals in all stages of their educational development:

- Adult learners
- College students
- Military personnel

Adult learners desiring college degrees face unique circumstances—demanding work schedules, family responsibilities, and tight budgets. Yet adult learners also have years of valuable work experience that can frequently be applied toward a degree through the DSST program. For example, adult learners with on-the-job experience in business and management might be able to skip the Business 101 courses if they earn passing marks on DSST exams such as Introduction to Business and Principles of Supervision.

Adult learners can put their prior learning into action and move forward with more advanced course work. Adults who have never enrolled in a college course may feel a little uncertain about their abilities. If this describes your situation, then sign up for a DSST exam and see how you do. A passing score may be the boost you need to realize your dream of earning a degree. With family and work commitments, adult learners often feel they lack the time to attend college. The DSST program enables adult learners the unique opportunity to work toward college degrees without the time constraints of semester-long course work. DSST exams take two hours or less to complete. In one weekend, you could earn credit for multiple college courses.

The DSST exams also benefit students who are already enrolled in a college or university. With college tuition costs on the rise, most students face financial challenges. The fee for each DSST exam starts at $80 (plus administration fees charged by some testing facilities)—significantly less than the $750 average cost of a 3-hour college class. Maximize tuition assistance by taking DSST exams for introductory or mandatory course work. Once you earn a passing score on a DSST exam, you are free to move on to higher-level course work in that subject matter, take desired electives, or focus on courses in a chosen major.

Not only do college students and adult learners profit from DSST exams, but military personnel reap the benefits as well. If you are a member of the armed services at home or abroad, you can initiate your post-military career by taking DSST exams in areas with which you have experience. Military personnel can gain credit anywhere in the world, thanks to the fact that almost all of the tests are available through the internet at designated testing locations. DSST testing facilities are located at more than 500 military installations, so service members on active duty can get a jump-start on a post-military career with the DSST program. As an additional incentive, DANTES (Defense Activity for Non-Traditional Education Support) provides funding for DSST test fees for eligible members of the military.

More than 30 subject-matter tests are available in the fields of Business, Humanities, Math, Physical Science, Social Sciences, and Technology.

Available DSST® Exams

Business	Social Sciences
Business Ethics and Society	A History of the Vietnam War
Business Mathematics	Art of the Western World
Computing and Information Technology	Criminal Justice
Human Resource Management	Foundations of Education
Introduction to Business	Fundamentals of Counseling
Management Information Systems	General Anthropology
Money and Banking	History of the Soviet Union
Organizational Behavior	Introduction to Geography
Personal Finance	Introduction to Law Enforcement
Principles of Finance	Lifespan Developmental Psychology
Principles of Supervision	Substance Abuse
	The Civil War and Reconstruction

Humanities	Physical Sciences
Ethics in America	Astronomy
Introduction to World Religions	Environmental Science
Principles of Advanced English	Health and Human Development
Composition	Introduction to Geology
Principles of Public Speaking	

Math	Technology
Fundamentals of College Algebra	Ethics in Technology
Math for Liberal Arts	Fundamentals of Cybersecurity
Principles of Statistics	Technical Writing

As you can see from the table, the DSST program covers a wide variety of subjects. However, it is important to ask two questions before registering for a DSST exam.

1. Which universities or colleges award credit for passing DSST exams?
2. Which DSST exams are the most relevant to my desired degree and my experience?

Knowing which universities offer DSST credit is important. In all likelihood, a college in your area awards credit for DSST exams, but find out before taking an exam by contacting the university directly. Then review the list of DSST exams to determine which ones are most relevant to the degree you are seeking and to your base of knowledge. Schedule an appointment with your college adviser to determine which exams best fit your degree program and which college courses the DSST exams can replace. Advisers should also be able to tell you the minimum score required on the DSST exam to receive university credit.

DSST® TEST CENTERS

You can find DSST testing locations in community colleges and universities across the country. Check the DSST website (**www.getcollegecredit. com**) for a location near you or contact your local college or university to find out if the school administers DSST exams. Keep in mind that some universities and colleges administer DSST exams only to enrolled students. DSST testing is available to men and women in the armed services at more than 500 military installations around the world.

HOW TO REGISTER FOR A DSST® EXAM

Once you have located a nearby DSST testing facility, you need to contact the testing center to find out the exam administration schedule. Many centers are set up to administer tests via the internet, while others use printed materials. Almost all DSST exams are available as online tests, but the method used depends on the testing center. The cost for each DSST exam starts at $80, and many testing locations charge a fee to cover their costs for administering the tests. Credit cards are the only accepted payment method for taking online DSST exams. Credit card, certified check, and money order are acceptable payment methods for paper-and-pencil tests.

Test takers are allotted two score reports—one mailed to them and another mailed to a designated college or university, if requested. Online tests generate unofficial scores at the end of the test session, while individuals taking paper tests must wait four to six weeks for score reports.

PREPARING FOR A DSST® EXAM

Even though you are knowledgeable in a certain subject matter, you should still prepare for the test to ensure you achieve the highest score possible. The first step in studying for a DSST exam is to find out what will be on the specific test you have chosen. Information regarding test content is located on the DSST fact sheets, which can be downloaded at no cost from **www.getcollegecredit.com**. Each fact sheet outlines the topics covered on a subject-matter test, as well as the approximate percentage assigned to each topic. For example, questions on the Criminal Justice exam are distributed in the following way: Criminal Behavior—15%, Criminal Justice System—25%, Law Enforcement—20%, Court System—20%, Corrections—20%.

In addition to the breakdown of topics on a DSST exam, the fact sheet also lists recommended reference materials. If you do not own the recommended books, then check college bookstores. Avoid paying high prices for new textbooks by looking online for used textbooks. Don't panic if you are unable to locate a specific textbook listed on the fact sheet; the textbooks are merely recommendations. Instead, search for comparable books used in university courses on the specific subject. Current editions are ideal, and it is a good idea to use at least two references when studying for a DSST exam. Of course, the subject matter provided in this book will be a sufficient review for most test takers. However, if you need additional information, then it is a good idea to have some of the reference materials at your disposal when preparing for a DSST exam.

Fact sheets include other useful information in addition to a list of reference materials and topics. Each fact sheet includes subject-specific sample questions like those you will encounter on the DSST exam. The sample questions provide an idea of the types of questions you can expect on the exam. Test questions are multiple-choice with one correct answer and three incorrect choices.

The fact sheet also includes information about the number of credit hours that ACE has recommended be awarded by colleges for a passing DSST exam score. However, you should keep in mind that not all universities and colleges adhere to the ACE recommendation for DSST credit hours. Some institutions require DSST exam scores higher than the minimum score recommended by ACE. Once you have acquired appropriate reference materials and you have the outline provided on the fact sheet, you are ready to start studying, which is where this book can help.

TEST DAY

After reviewing the material and taking practice tests, you are finally ready to take your DSST exam. Follow these tips for a successful test day experience.

1. **Arrive on time.** Not only is it courteous to arrive on time to the DSST testing facility, but it also allows plenty of time for you to take care of check-in procedures and settle into your surroundings.

2. **Bring identification.** DSST test facilities require that candidates bring a valid government-issued identification card with a current photo and signature. Acceptable forms of identification include a current driver's license, passport, military identification card, or state-issued identification card. Individuals who fail to bring proper identification to the DSST testing facility will not be allowed to take an exam.

3. **Bring the right supplies.** If your exam requires the use of a calculator, you may bring a calculator that meets the specifications. For paper-based exams, you may also bring No. 2 pencils with an eraser and black ballpoint pens. Regardless of the exam methodology, you are NOT allowed to bring reference or study materials, scratch paper, or electronics such as cell phones, personal handheld devices, cameras, alarm wrist watches, or tape recorders to the testing center.

4. **Take the test.** During the exam, take the time to read each question-and-answer option carefully. Eliminate the choices you know are incorrect to narrow the number of potential answers. If a question completely stumps you, take an educated guess and move on—remember that DSSTs are timed; you will have 2 hours to take the exam.

With the proper preparation, DSST exams will save you both time and money. So join the thousands of people who have already reaped the benefits of DSST exams and move closer than ever to your college degree.

CRIMINAL JUSTICE EXAM FACTS

The DSST® Criminal Justice exam consists of 100 multiple-choice questions that cover material commonly found in a college-level criminal justice course, including topics like criminal behavior; the roles of police and law enforcement at the federal, state and local levels; the US court system and its structures; sentencing issues; and the criminal justice system including adult prison systems and juvenile correction alternatives.

Area or Course Equivalent: Criminal Justice
Level: Lower-level baccalaureate
Amount of Credit: 3 Semester Hours
Minimum Score: 400
Source: https://www.getcollegecredit.com/wp-content/assets/factsheets /CriminalJustice.pdf

I. **Criminal Behavior – 15%**

   a. Defining crime (i.e., what is crime, accepted definitions of crime)

   b. Types of crime

   c. Juvenile delinquency (i.e., emergence, trends, causation)

   d. Measurement of crime and delinquency (i.e., UCR, NVCS, evaluation, survey data, research data, methods of data collection)

   e. Crime in the United states (i.e., rate, trends)

   f. Theories of crime

II. **Criminal Justice System – 25%**

   a. Historical origins and legal foundations (i.e., statutory, common law, case law, procedural and substantive law etc.)

   b. Crime control model versus due process model

   c. Criminal justice agencies (i.e., law enforcement, courts and corrections)

III. **Law Enforcement – 20%**

   a. History of policing

   b. Types of law enforcement agencies

   c. Law enforcement roles and responsibilities

   d. Issues and trends in policing

   e. The nature of law enforcement (i.e., PTSD, use of discretion, subculture and demographics (e.g., race, gender, age, etc.)

IV. **Court System – 20%**

   a. History of the court system

   b. Organization, structure and levels of the court system

   c. Adult and Juvenile court systems

    d. Pretrial, trial and post-trial processes (e.g., bail, plea bargaining, prosecutorial discretion, judicial discretion, diversion, waiver, jury, and verdict)

    e. Sentencing options and trends

V. Corrections – 20%

    a. History of corrections

    b. Philosophies of punishment (e.g., rehabilitation, restoration, deterrence, incapacitation, retribution)

    c. Intermediate sanctions (i.e., probation, parole)

    d. Adult prison facilities (i.e., administration and overcrowding)

    e. Juvenile correctional facilities (i.e., types, functions, and controversies)

    f. Capital punishment (i.e., controversies)

    g. Inmate characteristics (i.e., subculture, gangs and demographics)

    h. Issues and trends (i.e., inmate rights, security, healthcare, privatization and wrongful conviction)

Chapter 2

Criminal Justice Diagnostic Test

DIAGNOSTIC TEST ANSWER SHEET

1. Ⓐ Ⓑ Ⓒ Ⓓ	8. Ⓐ Ⓑ Ⓒ Ⓓ	15. Ⓐ Ⓑ Ⓒ Ⓓ
2. Ⓐ Ⓑ Ⓒ Ⓓ	9. Ⓐ Ⓑ Ⓒ Ⓓ	16. Ⓐ Ⓑ Ⓒ Ⓓ
3. Ⓐ Ⓑ Ⓒ Ⓓ	10. Ⓐ Ⓑ Ⓒ Ⓓ	17. Ⓐ Ⓑ Ⓒ Ⓓ
4. Ⓐ Ⓑ Ⓒ Ⓓ	11. Ⓐ Ⓑ Ⓒ Ⓓ	18. Ⓐ Ⓑ Ⓒ Ⓓ
5. Ⓐ Ⓑ Ⓒ Ⓓ	12. Ⓐ Ⓑ Ⓒ Ⓓ	19. Ⓐ Ⓑ Ⓒ Ⓓ
6. Ⓐ Ⓑ Ⓒ Ⓓ	13. Ⓐ Ⓑ Ⓒ Ⓓ	20. Ⓐ Ⓑ Ⓒ Ⓓ
7. Ⓐ Ⓑ Ⓒ Ⓓ	14. Ⓐ Ⓑ Ⓒ Ⓓ	

CRIMINAL JUSTICE DIAGNOSTIC TEST

Directions: Carefully read each of the following 20 questions. Choose the best answer to each question and fill in the corresponding circle on the answer sheet. The Answer Key and Explanations can be found following this Diagnostic Test.

1. Crimes that are considered to be wrong by their very nature, such as assaults, theft, and murder are called

    A. mala prohibita.
    B. felonies.
    C. mala in se.
    D. organized crime.

2. Which theory states that being around criminal behavior influences an individual towards criminality?

    A. Biological theory
    B. Learning theory
    C. Labeling theory
    D. Psychological theory

3. A crime report that is generated on a yearly basis by the FBI for a statistical analysis and summary is called the

    A. dark figure of crime.
    B. UCR.
    C. NIBRS.
    D. NCVS.

4. The notion of a guilty state of mind is defined by which term?

    A. Mala in se
    B. Mens rea
    C. Retribution
    D. Probable cause

5. The notion that a person has the right to protect themselves from self-incrimination is found in the

   A. Fifth Amendment.
   B. Fourth Amendment.
   C. First Amendment.
   D. Eighth Amendment.

6. The right to counsel and to a speedy and public trial falls under the

   A. Sixth Amendment.
   B. Eighth Amendment.
   C. Fifth Amendment.
   D. Fourth Amendment.

7. The standard to convict an individual in criminal court is

   A. reasonable suspicion.
   B. probable cause.
   C. beyond a reasonable doubt.
   D. preponderance of the evidence.

8. The agency within the criminal justice system that is responsible for due process and sentencing offenders under the sentencing laws and guidelines is

   A. corrections.
   B. the judicial branch.
   C. law enforcement.
   D. the parole board.

9. When Sir Robert Peel created the first London police force in 1829, the officers were called

   A. coppers.
   B. Londoners.
   C. bobbies.
   D. peelers.

10. Which years encompass the Community Policing Era, which has a focus on police community relations, where police assist with social service calls?

A. 1840-1920
B. 1920-1970
C. 1970–present
D. 2001–present

11. Law enforcement changes and evolves as it reflects societal needs. One of the major issues that law enforcement is facing present day is

A. traffic control.
B. sentencing of violent offenders.
C. antiterrorism.
D. auto larceny.

12. Law enforcement contains a high level of stress due to the nature of its work. A common result of stress that police officers face is

A. high suicide rates among officers.
B. divorce.
C. alcohol abuse.
D. All of the above

13. The Judiciary Act, passed in 1789, created which court?

A. Criminal court
B. Civil court
C. Family court
D. The Supreme Court

14. On a state level, the courts that handle misdemeanor cases and civil lawsuits up to a certain amount of money are known as

A. courts of general jurisdiction.
B. civil courts.
C. Supreme Courts.
D. courts of limited jurisdiction.

15. The judicial system is divided into an adult and juvenile court system. In the adult court system, the accused is known as the

    A. offender.
    B. perpetrator.
    C. complainant.
    D. defendant.

16. A grand jury can be convened to hear and review serious criminal offenses. If the grand jury determines probable cause, the next step for the defendant is

    A. initial appearance.
    B. sentencing.
    C. bail.
    D. arraignment.

17. One of the main principles of corrections in the United States is deterrence to control people's behavior. What are the two types of deterrence?

    A. General and specific
    B. Individual and community
    C. Incorporation and rehabilitation
    D. General and rehabilitation

18. The adult prison system is intended for individuals 18 years and older. Its main purpose is

    A. restitution.
    B. rehabilitation.
    C. punishment.
    D. retribution.

19. Which of the following are residential treatment programs within the juvenile system?

    A. Group homes
    B. Foster care
    C. Family group homes
    D. All of the above

20. Which amendment challenges the constitutionality of the death penalty as well as the methods of execution?

A. Fourth Amendment
B. Second Amendment
C. Fifth Amendment
D. Eighth Amendment

ANSWER KEY AND EXPLANATIONS

1. C	5. A	9. C	13. D	17. A
2. B	6. A	10. C	14. D	18. C
3. B	7. C	11. C	15. D	19. D
4. B	8. B	12. D	16. D	20. D

1. **The correct answer is C.** *Mala in se* offenses are offenses that are wrong by their very own nature. Choice A is incorrect because *mala prohibita* crimes are prohibited by law, but may not be wrong in and of themselves. Choice B is incorrect because a felony is a classification of crime used to determine punishment. Choice D is incorrect because organized crime is a category of crime signifying organizations of smaller criminal networks.

2. **The correct answer is B.** Learning theory, suggested by Edwin Sutherland, states that values associated with deviant behavior are learned through interaction with family and friends. Choice A is incorrect because the biological theory refers to the idea that people have a genetic makeup for deviant behavior. Choice C is incorrect because the labeling theory believes that society creates deviance by creating rules. Choice D is incorrect because psychological theory states that deviant behavior can be found in those with personality conditions.

3. **The correct answer is B.** The Uniform Crime Report (UCR) is generated yearly after compiling statistics from local, state, and federal law enforcement agencies. Choice A is incorrect because the dark figure of crime is not a statistical analysis, but rather a component of crime that is not reported. Choice C is incorrect because the NIBRS is the National Incident-Based Reporting System, which is used by police officers when reporting more than one offense in a criminal incident. Choice D is incorrect because the NCVS is the National Crime Victimization Survey, which is used as a self-reporting survey for individuals who were victims of a crime.

4. **The correct answer is B.** Mens rea refers to the guilty state of mind. The term is derived from common law during colonial times. Choice A is incorrect because mala in se are offenses that are wrong in and of themselves. Choice C is incorrect because retribution is based on revenge and punishment. Choice D is incorrect because probable cause is a standard for an arrest.

5. **The correct answer is A.** The Fifth Amendment protects individuals from being forced by the State to answer questions that may incriminate themselves. Choice B is incorrect because the Fourth Amendment prohibits unreasonable searches and seizures. Choice C is incorrect because the First Amendment guarantees freedom of speech. Choice D is incorrect because the Eighth Amendment prohibits cruel and unusual punishment.

6. **The correct answer is A.** The Sixth Amendment covers a person's right to counsel as well as a speedy and public trial. Choice B is incorrect because the Eighth Amendment deals with cruel and unusual punishment. Choice C is incorrect because the Fifth Amendment is about double jeopardy and self-incrimination. Choice D is incorrect because the Fourth Amendment deals with unreasonable searches and seizure.

7. **The correct answer is C.** Beyond a reasonable doubt is the legal standard for conviction in criminal court. Choice A is incorrect because reasonable suspicion is a standard for police to conduct stops and question people. Choice B is incorrect because probable cause is the standard for an arrest. Choice D is incorrect because the preponderance of evidence is used in a civil court proceeding.

8. **The correct answer is B.** The judicial branch has the responsibility through the courts to establish guilt or innocence through due process and hand down sentencing for guilty offenders. Choice A is incorrect because corrections departments enforce the sentencing by the courts. Choice C is incorrect because law enforcement is an overarching term for all that goes into enforcing the laws of the land and maintaining order. Choice D is incorrect because a parole board decides whether or not an offender should be released from prison.

9. **The correct answer is C.** The origin of the name "bobbies" for London police officers is derived from Sir Robert Peel's name. Therefore, choices A, B, and D are all incorrect.

10. **The correct answer is C.** The Community Policing Era picked up where the Professional Era ended in 1970, and continues to present day. Choice A is incorrect because 1840-1920 was the Political Era. Choice B is incorrect because 1920-1970 was the Professional Era. Choice D is incorrect because there is no defined era within that time span.

11. **The correct answer is C.** Since 9/11, policing in America has changed and departments and officers must be extremely vigilant in the fight against terrorism. Choice A is incorrect because traffic control has always been a police-related issue. Choice B is incorrect because this is not a police function at all, but a judicial issue within the court system. Choice D is incorrect because auto larceny is a crime that occurs on a regular basis, and the police have always combatted auto larceny as part of routine police work.

12. **The correct answer is D.** Because of the high level of stress that police officers face, they commonly fall prey to all of the listed choices.

13. **The correct answer is D.** The Judiciary Act created the Supreme Court, which then consisted of a Chief Justice and five Associate Justices.

14. **The correct answer is D.** Courts of limited jurisdiction only hear misdemeanor cases and, depending on the state, civil cases for small amounts of money. Choice A is incorrect because courts of general jurisdiction hear felony cases and civil cases for larger sums of money. Choice B is incorrect because civil courts do not hear any criminal cases. Choice C is incorrect because the Supreme Court hears cases involving Constitutional issues.

15. **The correct answer is D.** In adult court, the individual accused of a crime is known as the defendant.

16. **The correct answer is D.** Arraignment takes place after a grand jury has established probable cause; there, the defendant is brought before the judge to hear the charges that were found against him. Therefore, choices A, B and C are all incorrect because they are other steps within the judicial process.

17. **The correct answer is A.** General and specific are the two types of deterrence. General deterrence prevents criminal behavior within a society. Specific deterrence targets the behavior of the individual offender.

18. **The correct answer is C.** The adult prison system is intended for punishment. Choice A is incorrect; restitution is part of corrections, but it is not part of the prison system. Choice B is incorrect because adult prison systems have fewer vocational and educational services than juvenile facilities. Choice D is incorrect because although retribution is a goal of corrections, it is not specific to adults and can be applied to any age group in which the punishment fits the crime.

19. **The correct answer is D.** Group homes, foster homes, and family homes are all part of juvenile treatment programs.

20. **The correct answer is D.** The Eighth Amendment challenges not only the death penalty but also the methods that are used for execution under the cruel and unusual punishment clause. Therefore, choices A, B and C are all incorrect as they do not relate to cruel and unusual punishment.

DIAGNOSTIC TEST ASSESSMENT GRID

Now that you've completed the diagnostic test and read through the answer explanations, you can use your results to target your studying. Find the question numbers from the diagnostic test that you answered incorrectly and highlight or circle them below. Then focus extra attention on the sections dealing with those topics.

Criminal Justice

Content Area	Topic	Question #
Criminal Behavior	• Defining Crime • Types of Crime • Theories of Crime • Measurement of Crime • Juvenile Delinquency	1, 2, 3
Criminal Justice System	• Historical Origins • Legal Foundations • Due Process • Criminal Justice Agencies	4, 5, 6, 7, 8
Law Enforcement	• History of Policing • Law Enforcement Roles & Responsibilities • Issues and Trends in Policing • The Nature of Law Enforcement	9, 10, 11, 12
Courts	• History of the Court System • Organization and Structure • Adult Court System • Juvenile Court	13, 14, 15
Court System	• Pretrial, Trial, and Post-Trial Process	16
Corrections	• Purpose • Intermediate Sanctions • Juvenile Correction Alternatives • Capital Punishment • Prison Organization • Prison Subculture	17, 18, 19, 20

Chapter 3

Criminal Justice Subject Review

This chapter reviews all the topics you'll see on your DSST Criminal Justice exam. The American criminal justice system is a large, complex, and vital institution that includes a variety of interconnected subsystems. It is one of the oldest institutions in America's history and is the cornerstone of its democracy. The criminal justice system, as with many other intuitions, has grown and evolved over time.

Because the criminal justice system is so complex, many people don't realize how interwoven it is within American society, and how it affects everyday lives. People outside of the criminal justice system think they have an idea about how the system works based on the news, television, movies, and social media. All of these variables may help shape people's beliefs and opinions about the criminal justice system, both in negative and positive ways—in reality, most of these depictions don't accurately portray the criminal justice system or its various agencies and personnel.

Why is this so important? People's beliefs and opinions about the effectiveness of the criminal justice process can affect its practices, policies, and conduct at all levels.

This chapter will help you understand the various levels and agencies that comprise the criminal justice system and prepare you for exam day.

You'll get an overview of how the criminal justice system operates, along with the various roles and parts of the system, with the understanding that each component is more complex than the general review provided here. The topics covered include criminal behavior, what defines it, how it's measured, the different types of crimes, and the different theories behind criminality and deviant behavior. We'll also examine the historical perspective of the criminal justice system within a legal framework, including due process.

Different agencies are also examined, including the police and how they're organized, as well as some of the issues and trends that today's police officers face. Additionally, we look at the occupational characteristics of police officers in today's society.

The court system is the next tier that will be covered, including its history and origin, and how it's structured—from the adult system to the juvenile system. The trial process will also be examined, along with the various sentencing issues and trends that the American court system faces.

The last part of the criminal justice system we'll cover is sometimes the least recognizable—corrections. How does corrections fit into American society and what is its role and purpose within the criminal justice system? Finally, we'll look into how prisons operate and what takes place behind their walls and bars.

CRIMINAL BEHAVIOR

Defining Crime

Let's start with a basic definition. When asked to define *crime*, most people would simply say that it means breaking laws that have been written and established by elected officials. While this is partially correct, defining crime is a little more involved and complex. The formal definition of crime according to the manual *The American System of Criminal Justice* is as follows:

> *A specific act of commission or omission in violation of the law, where a punishment is prescribed*

Let's examine the part of the definition that states "… act of commission … " Commission entails *doing* something. If I took a baseball bat and hit you with it, it would be an act of assault; if I stole your car, it would be an act of larceny. That's the easy part to understand—performing an act in violation of the law. The other part of the definition states "… act of commission *or omission…*" If commission means doing, then omission means *not* doing something. How does not doing something violate the law? Here's an example: the police, hospitals, and schools all have a mandatory reporting requirement for suspected child abuse. If someone from one of these agencies *fails* to report it, then that is a crime. Other examples include the failure to file your taxes—a crime of *not* doing something that's required by law. If you had a court date and *failed* to show up for your required appearance that would also be an omission—and would result in a court ordered bench warrant.

Finally, the definition and concept of crime must include some sort of pre-scribed punishment. In order for the law to work, punishment must be attached—it does not matter what the punishment is, just that there is a pre-scribed punishment. That being said, crimes need to be written down and codified, most likely in the penal law, in order to define which acts are illegal.

Crimes can be defined in two ways:

1. The first is **mala in se**. This means offenses that are wrong by their very nature—for example, murder, rape, robbery, and assault. We know just by the acts that they are immoral and wrong.
2. Next is **mala prohibita**. Here, the law prohibits certain offenses, but they are *not* wrong in and of themselves. This refers to crimes like gambling, drug use, and prostitution in some circumstances, or even minor infractions like speeding.

Crime in The United States

Crime in the United States follows particular trends and patterns, which are statistically compiled and classified across the country. Interestingly, the perception of crime may be different from what the actual statistics show. Let's examine some studies about crime trends from the past few years.

The Uniform Crime Reporting (UCR) Program shows that during the first 6 months of 2015, compared to 2014, violent crime was up by 1.7 percent, while property crime went down by 4.2 percent. In 2016, violent crimes increased by 4.1 percent and property crimes decreased by 1.3 percent from the previous year.

Some reports released for 2015 stated that crime levels remained the same from the prior year. That being said, even as crime levels off and sometimes declines, there are still increases in certain cities, and in specific crimes. As reported by *U.S. News & World Report*, the United States has seen historic decreases in overall crime. However, in 2015, even as crime remained at an all-time low, there was a slight increase in violent crimes compared to 2014. As per *U.S. News & World Report*, violent crime rose 3.9 percent across the entire year compared to 2014. This was largely attributed to gang violence and shootings. The murder rate also showed an increase nationwide—how-ever, only three cities were largely responsible for this increase: Baltimore, Chicago, and Washington, D.C.

Still, overall crime appears to be on the decrease and at an all-time low, even as crime levels increase in Chicago, Charlotte, and Los Angeles and skew the national average. Statistics also indicate that males in the age range of 15 to 24 commit the majority of crimes nationwide.

Geography and race are key factors in tracking trends and patterns of crime, with violent crimes occurring more frequently in urban areas. The Uniform Crime Report also breaks down violent crime categories in cities with populations of 100,000 or more—the report shows a statistical significance between large cities with lower socioeconomic populations and violent crimes, including murder. Available statistics also demonstrate that most violent crimes are **intraracial**, meaning that both victims and offenders are from the same race.

Theories of Crime

For years, criminologists have pondered what causes crime. There are many theories—let's examine a few of the most popular ones, including the two primary schools of thought in the field of criminology.

Classical Criminology

Classical criminology views behavior as stemming from free will, and demands responsibility and accountability for all offenders. Punishment is a key factor in this theory; it demands punishment to deter individuals from committing further deviant acts. In order for this theory to function properly, the punishment needs to be predictable. This theory is applied in modern court procedures and philosophy. The American court system, for the most part, holds offenders accountable for their actions.

During the Age of Enlightenment, also known as the Age of Reason, social reformers enacted changes throughout society regarding crime and punishment. The prior Draconian methods of torture used to influence behavior began to shift towards more humane methods of punishment. The two most influential theorists in this field during the Age of Enlightenment were Cesare Beccaria and Jeremy Bentham.

Cesare Beccaria was an 18th century criminologist who believed in classical criminology. Beccaria wrote a famous book, *An Essay on Crimes and Punishment*, which essentially states that behavior stems from free will and people are accountable for their behavior. The book supports the notion that societies should protect themselves by preventing crime. Beccaria also believed the following ideas:

- Criminal behavior is rational; people choose to commit crimes after weighing out the pros and cons, and fear of punishment keeps people in check.
- Crime is an injury to society and people need to be punished accordingly.
- The accused has the right to a speedy trial and to bring forth evidence on his or her behalf.
- The purpose of punishment is deterrence.
- Swiftness of punishment is more important than its severity.
- Prisons should be more humane, with clear prisoner classifications based on age, sex, and the degree of the offense.

Jeremey Bentham was one of the great English thinkers regarding criminal law, and was known for his utilitarian philosophy. **Utilitarianism** is defined as the greatest possible balance of pleasure over pain, and that determining whether actions are morally right or wrong depends on the effects and results that they produce.

Utilitarianism believes that people behave in ways that bring about the greatest pleasure and avoid pain. Bentham, a reformer, emphasized deterrence and prevention (people seek to avoid pain and unpleasantness) in his views of crime and punishment.

Positivist Criminology

On the other side of the spectrum is the **positivist theory of criminology**, which views behavior as stemming from sociological, biological, and psychological factors. Proponents of this theory believe that punishment should be tailored to fit the individual and not the crime, that human behavior is controlled, and that there is no free will and no personal responsibility. Positivist criminologists use science to study crime and treat deviants, and believe that criminals have a different makeup than noncriminals.

One of the most famous biological criminologists was **Cesare Lombroso**, who felt there was a biological explanation for committing crimes. Lombroso believed that looking at people's physical traits could allow you to distinguish criminals from noncriminals—in other words, people are born criminals based on their physical genetic makeup. Lombroso, who visited insane asylums and other institutions for subjects, would measure and record people's physical traits. Some of the traits that he linked to criminal behavior included the size of a person's skull and forehead, deep-set eyes, an oversized nose, and large hands and fingers, among others.

The notion of criminality being linked to biological factors did not stop at Lombroso. Other psychologists also attempted to link deviant behavior to physical characteristics, including William Sheldon. Under the positivist explanation of deviant behavior, Sheldon created different categories that united or linked the biological and psychological makeups of individuals and behavior. These classifications included three different and distinct body types:

Endomorphs: People who are round and soft had a tendency towards a "viscerotonic" type of personality, which means someone who is relaxed, comfortable, and considered an extrovert.

Mesomorphs: People who are square and muscular and who have tendencies towards a "somotonic" personality, which means someone who is active, assertive, and aggressive.

Ectomorphs: These are people who are thin and believed to have a tendency towards a "cerebrotonic" personality, which is someone who is introverted, thoughtful, and sensitive.

Sheldon used these classification systems to explain deviant behavior. He claimed that criminality and delinquency are derived from the mesomorphic category. His theory was that individuals who are firmly in the mesomorphic category are aggressive and lack sensitivity, and tend to exhibit criminal behavior.

Over time, as modern science and medicine became more advanced, the notion of linking physical traits and criminality did not withstand the test of time. Sheldon's theory, which at the time was considered innovative, later on became unsubstantiated as well.

The more modern biological explanation for deviant behavior looks at biological factors that predispose some people to exhibit criminal behavior. This theory relies on genetic makeup, which proponents say outweighs other social factors. One theory, called the **XYY chromosome theory**, is based on the premise that males who are born with an extra Y chromosome are more likely predisposed to deviant behavior and criminality.

Today's research investigates the notion of a link between genetic makeup and deviant behavior, and the connection with biological and environmental factors. Also under investigation is the notion of how injuries, such as head trauma, may affect behavior.

Psychological Theories

Let's discuss some of the primary psychological theories regarding why individuals commit crimes.

One of the most prominent theorists and psychologists in the world was **Sigmund Freud**. Freud was, and still is, one of the most famous, respected, and controversial figures in psychology. Among his many theories explaining human behavior is the **psychodynamic theory**. This theory suggests that unconscious forces and drives formed from early childhood control a person's personality and behavior. Freud believed that certain elements make up human personality and behavior. These elements are called the id, ego, and superego.

- The **id** is found in a person's unconscious self at birth. According to Freud, it drives the urges for food, sex, and other life necessities. The id's main concern is instant gratification. For example, a baby cries when he is hungry, thirsty, or needs to be changed. Freud does not say that a baby has immediate sexual desires to be fulfilled; rather, he is stating that those drives and urges are there and are buried, and have to be nurtured and developed.
- The **ego** balances out the id, trying to realistically satisfy its needs in a manner that is appropriate for society. When people develop an ego, they learn that the id cannot always be instantly gratified and compensated. This begins in early childhood.
- The **superego** provides people with a set of moral standards—in other words, your conscience, which is formed by your home environment during your formative years and society. The superego helps with judgment in determining right from wrong.

So, how does this relate to criminality? Freud's theory states that if the ego and/or the superego are not developed properly (for example, due to poor or absent parenting) then deviant behavior can arise. If the ego is damaged, the id takes over with impulsive behavior. If the superego is damaged, then there is no sense of morality and right from wrong.

Sociological Theories

Sociological explanations for criminality suggest that social conditions can affect individuals enough to cause criminal behavior. In other words, criminals are made by external factors.

Social Process Theories

Social process theories suggest that everyone has the potential to become a criminal depending on the following:

- The influences that drive a person towards or away from crime
- How one is regarded by others in his or her life

Edwin Sutherland was a criminologist who suggested that criminal behavior, like other behavioral traits, is learned through interaction with family and friends. Sutherland believed that people learn values and behaviors that are associated with crime. This is also known as the **differential association theory**, or the **learning theory**.

Sutherland believed that people learn values, attitudes, and motives by interacting with others. When it comes to criminality, a person "learns" how to become a criminal. In addition, there are many factors behind Sutherland's differential association theory that are taken into consideration, such as a person's socioeconomic background.

His theory can be explained through certain key points and assumptions:

- Criminal behavior is a learned behavior.
- The learning process for criminal behavior occurs through intimate personal relationships with others.
- The learning process for criminal behavior can be taught through techniques regarding how to commit crimes.
- People choose to become criminals because the favorable conclusions for committing a crime are more valued than the potential unfavorable conclusions.

Criminologists who subscribe to the **control theory** propose that criminal behavior occurs when the bonds that tie an individual to society are weakened or broken. These ties are often formed in family, church, and school. When these ties are broken, a person is more inclined to commit deviant behavior.

Labeling theory states that criminal behavior is not found in the individual; instead, crime is socially constructed. Society creates deviance by making rules and applying them to itself. When an individual acts a certain way, they are then perceived to be deviant and labeled as such, and this has the effect of a self-fulfilling prophecy on current and future behavior.

Emile Durkheim and **Robert Merton** believed in a theory called anomie. **Anomie** is defined as a breakdown in, and the disappearance of, the rules of social behavior. When the rules and norms that guide behavior are weakened or disappear, the result is deviant behavior.

Types of Crime

Different categories of crime have been established over the course of time. To help us understand these categories, let's start with some common definitions.

A **felony** is a crime carrying a penalty that ranges from incarceration for a minimum of one year to the death penalty.

A **misdemeanor** is a crime carrying a penalty of incarceration for no more than a year.

We know that there are hundreds of types of crimes under state or federal law; these include murder, manslaughter, larceny, assault, sexual assault, drug offenses, trespassing, and many more.

Let's examine some additional categories of crime:

Visible crime is defined as street crime or ordinary crime that can be observed and is usually most upsetting to the public. This does not literally mean you have to actually see the crime occur. It refers to such crimes as shoplifting, vandalism, and homicide.

Occupational crime is created through opportunities in an otherwise legal or legitimate business or occupation. For example, if you are a cashier at a supermarket, that is a legitimate job. But if you steal money out of the register while working, that is occupational crime, or white-collar crime. Edwin Sutherland developed this concept. Bribes, thefts by employees, and insider trading are all occupational crime.

Organized crime includes criminal acts in the fields of gambling, drugs, and prostitution that can be found through entities like the Mafia. There are many types of crime organizations, such as drug cartels. These entities have a structure and run like a business. One of the mechanisms that these organizations use is money laundering, which entails taking the profits from crime and filtering it through a legal business to make it clean so authorities cannot trace it.

Crimes without victims involve exchanges of illegal goods or services that are in strong demand in society. As a result, society as a whole is being injured, not one particular person. These crimes can overlap with organized crime, as well. Some of these crimes carry a moral weight. Is prostitution a victimless crime? Who is being harmed? And what about drug use? These are all debatable issues.

Political crime involves ideological issues or, in other words, crimes against the state. Terrorist acts fall under this label. These are not bribes to politicians—those are occupational crimes since being a politician is a legitimate occupation. Rather, these are crimes against a state or government.

Cybercrime includes offenses involving the use of computers, such as hacking into computer databanks or setting up viruses to damage computers or computer systems.

Measuring crime levels and analyzing crime statistics is an extremely valuable tool in the criminal justice system. This information can show us key national trends in crime; at the same time, we can follow local crime statistics to examine if crime in a city or neighborhood is on the rise or decline, and what categories are increasing or decreasing. Crime reporting is also a very useful tool for crime detection and follow-up investigations. The criminal justice system relies on crime reports and statistics.

The Dark Figure of Crime

Before we get into reporting techniques, let's expand upon a key concept: **the dark figure of crime**. The dark figure of crime is a dimension of crime that is never reported to the police. This is not to say that the crime never took place, it was just never reported or recorded. It does not matter what the crime is, or how big or small—people will have many different reasons for not reporting it to the police.

If someone breaks into a car and steals a smartphone, it may not be worth the person's time and may be more of an inconvenience to them to file a report. Unfortunately, for a more serious crime like rape, the victim may feel ashamed or responsible, and does not want to face what might arise when reporting this crime.

Other issues arise when determining whether or not to report a crime. First, someone might fail to recognize that a crime has been committed. For instance, for crimes that involve fraud, the victim may not even realize that he or she was a victim of a fraudulent scheme.

Another factor of the dark figure of crime is when an incident is reported to the police but isn't processed. If a complainant calls the police and says that her car window was broken, the police may try to avoid the report by telling the car owner that her premiums might go up if the report goes to the insurance company. The complainant may then opt out of reporting the incident and decide to get the damages fixed out of pocket.

Another factor in the dark figure of crime is how the police classifies an incident. This type of scenario can go a couple of different ways. Depending on the incident, the police may take the report and reclassify the crime, perhaps even downgrading it, which affects crime statistics. Even though a crime is being reported the police might reclassify the incident, which may not lead to an accurate report. This type of practice has been monitored and addressed by police departments, and the process of correctly classifying crimes continues to evolve.

Measurement of Crime

When a crime report is completed and inputted, it becomes part of the **National Incident-Based Reporting System**, or **NIBRS**. In this report, the police officer details each offense that was committed during the crime. For example, if someone is robbed at gunpoint and also assaulted, although the robbery is the most severe charge, the assault and weapons charges are key and must be noted as well.

The NIBRS is a nationally recognized and utilized reporting system for police departments throughout the country. Any law enforcement agency that wants to use the NIBRS has to submit its request to the FBI. The law enforcement agency has to submit the structure of the report, crime categories, number of offenses collected per incident, and data values for incidents, which will then be reviewed for approval by the FBI.

National crime reports, called the **Uniform Crime Reports** or **UCR**, are updated and published every year by the FBI. All local police departments, including local, state, federal, and tribal departments, have to report their yearly statistics to the FBI. The FBI studies and analyzes these statistics and publishes these reports to the public. These reports are broken down into statistical categories, which allow us to analyze trends and patterns in crime.

Crimes reported to the FBI are put into categories, called Index Crimes. They include the following:

- Murder
- Burglary
- Rape
- Grand larceny

- Robbery
- Grand larceny, auto
- Felony assaults
- Arson

The UCR is extremely helpful and accurate, but because of the dark figure of crime, it may provide an incomplete picture of crime trends. In order to close the gap between the UCR and the dark figure of crime, the United States Department of Justice created the **National Crime Victimization Survey (NCVS)** in 1972.

The Department of Justice uses the Bureau of Justice Statistics to send out surveys two times a year to determine the number and types of crimes and victims that went unreported, in addition to reported incidents. Over the years, the surveys have been reorganized and are still used today by the Department of Justice to build a crime index.

The NCVS samples approximately 90,000 households and 160,000 people. It collects information on crimes that fall into the UCR's list of Index Crimes, with the exception of murder. The survey includes victims who experienced crime but did not report these crimes to the police.

The NCVS asks recipients to provide information about themselves, including age, sex, race, marital status, education, and income level. It also asks for any information about the offender as well, when available. The victim also answers questions as to why they reported, or did not report, the incident to the police.

Juvenile Delinquency

Juvenile delinquency is criminal behavior committed by a minor who falls under a particular age. What is most interesting and concerning about juvenile delinquency is how the criminal justice system finds ways to manage these young members of society, and the ever-changing philosophies about the causes of delinquency and the punishments that should be administered.

Let's examine some of the modern ideas about trends that can lead a young person to delinquency. The state of the economy and job market has always exhibited a correlation between juvenile delinquency and criminality in general. Let's assume that a poor economy or job rate leads to criminality in general. How does this relate to delinquency? The lack of availability of after-school jobs, and the structure and responsibility they provide, may drive kids to deviant behavior.

Other correlates for juvenile delinquency may exist in the social arena. As societies become more complex, something close to what we see in anomie tends to occur—more social issues develop and people, particularly kids, must encounter these issues on a daily basis without the maturity to know how to deal with them properly. These may include racial conflicts, physical or cyber-bullying, and the lure and power of social media.

Drug use has always been a common cause of juvenile delinquency. The rise of drug epidemics over the years, in connection with a poor economy, leaves time and opportunity for juveniles to become involved in delinquent behavior, including drug trafficking, turf wars among rival gangs that sell drugs, and increased street violence. Also, the social trend of designer drugs can lead to higher consumption by minors, leading to delinquency and deviant behavior.

Gangs and gang activity have a direct correlation with the rise of juvenile delinquency. It's estimated that there are approximately 800,000 gang members nationwide. Violence and weapons are typical in the lives of gang members, which of course lead to acts of criminal behavior. Research indicates that gangs fall into four categories.

- **Social gangs:** Members are involved in few delinquent acts including some drug use (with the exception of some marijuana and alcohol). Social gang members are more interested in social activities.
- **Party gangs:** Members concentrate on drug use and sales to support themselves and their personal use; there is little delinquent behavior in this group.
- **Serious delinquent gangs:** Members engage in serious delinquent acts and criminal behavior; drug dealing is not their main objective and drug use is typically for personal use.
- **Organized gangs:** Members are extremely involved in criminal behavior; drug use and sales are connected with other criminal acts; and violence is used to establish control over territory for drug sales and distribution. These gangs are very organized and can become formal criminal enterprises.

The average age of gang members has been changing in recent times; today, gang members may be as old as 55 or older. This indicates that gang members are staying with their gangs longer.

Gang research shows that young people can be involved with gangs as early as age 9, and by the time they're 12 can be full gang members. At the ages of 10 and 11, they have often committed some violent acts for initiation. By the age of 13, they may have fired their first gun, seen someone get killed, gotten their first tattoo, or been arrested.

Gangs have also seen an increase in female members. Some of the reasons may include financial opportunities through drug sales and theft, enhanced perception of identity and status, peer pressure, and broken families. Another possible reason could be for the excitement they get from belonging to a gang.

According to the National Youth Gang Survey, most gangs are made up of members with predominately black and Hispanic backgrounds. The average ethnic breakdown is as follows:

- Hispanic: 49 percent
- Black: 35 percent
- White: 9 percent
- Asian/Other: 7 percent

Gangs can also be broken down geographically. For instance, in Philadelphia and Detroit the majority of gang members are black. In New York and Los Angeles, gang members are mostly Hispanic.

Let's now look at what happens when accused criminals enter the criminal justice system. What are their rights? How does the system ensure a fair and just process?

THE CRIMINAL JUSTICE SYSTEM

The ideas that comprise the criminal justice system date back to Biblical times and the B.C. era, and come from all parts of the world. It has evolved over time and continues to evolve and grow, but there are still some core underlying principles regarding crime and punishment.

Historical Origins and Legal Foundations

One of the earliest and most famous laws is the **Hammurabi code** (1750 B.C.E.). These were Babylonian laws written and codified to help keep the gods happy, and were based on the principle of retribution. **Retribution** is essentially payback—the idea that offenders need to be punished. Hammurabi had the notion to inflict pain unto offenders as they had to their victims. This pain is not necessarily physical; it also includes financial punishment. These laws dealt with all forms of societal behavior. The standard for these laws was based on "**lex talionis**," the notion of "an eye for an eye." For instance, if you broke somebody's bone, he would break your bone. If you were caught committing a robbery, the punishment was death.

As time passed, the criminal justice system evolved all over the world, and the United States was no exception. The origins of the criminal justice system in America derived from English tradition. During colonial times, the criminal justice system was based on common law and the notion of **mens rea**, which refers to a guilty mind, or knowledge of wrongdoing. The Catholic church also helped to guide and shape human behavior, values, and morals. The colonies used common law, based on judges' previous rulings and decisions, to assist or guide them, as there were no codified or written laws on the books.

These colonial laws were later reshaped and modified by William Penn. Prior to the Revolutionary War, Penn realized that there had to be a humane and compassionate component to the system. He believed in housing and rehabilitation for offenders and set up the first bail system.

Following the Revolutionary War, the creation of the U.S. Constitution led to equal rights and protections for citizens, and punishment for criminal offenders. In the early 1900s, Theodore Roosevelt helped usher in Progressive Era reform to the criminal justice system, and helped create national law enforcement agencies such as the FBI. Sentencing laws were also created during this time, along with the juvenile justice system.

Due Process

The American criminal justice system is built upon the notion of **due process**. Due process is fair treatment in all legal matters, whether civil or criminal. The concept of due process can be found in the Fifth Amendment of the Constitution, which states that no person shall be deprived of life, liberty, or property without having notice and a chance to present his or her side. The due process clause is also attached to the Fourteenth Amendment, which later applied these legal rights to all states as well.

Due process actually limits the powers of the state and federal governments, and requires them to follow certain procedural rules and laws. In addition, the responsibility to convict an individual of a crime in a criminal proceeding is placed upon the government or state, which must reach the standard that a person is guilty beyond a reasonable doubt.

In essence, due process grants the populace the protections of life, liberty, and property. But where do these protections come from and how are they applied? They are actually found in particular amendments to the **Bill of Rights**, the first 10 amendments of the U.S. Constitution. Let's take a closer look at some of the amendments that apply directly to criminal justice.

The **Fourth Amendment** includes the rights of people to be secure in their persons, houses, papers, and effects against unreasonable searches and seizures, and that no warrants shall be issued without probable cause.

The Fourth Amendment does give way to certain exceptions regarding police search and seizure, in specific cases. However, if the courts determine that the police acted unfairly or violated the Fourth Amendment clause and evidence was illegally seized, it would fall under the exclusionary rule.

The **exclusionary rule** states that when evidence is illegally obtained in searches and seizures it must be excluded from trial. In other words, the evidence would not be admissible at trial. This is also called "The Fruit of the Poisonous Tree" doctrine.

The **Fifth Amendment** protects the public from what is called double jeopardy—it stops prosecutors from subjecting a person to prosecution more than once in the same jurisdiction for the same offense. The Fifth Amendment also addresses self-incrimination, which simply means that the state cannot force someone to answer questions about himself or herself that may reveal a criminal act.

The **Sixth Amendment** includes the right to counsel and to a speedy and public trial, the right to confront witnesses, and the right to an impartial jury. This amendment ensures that there are no closed proceedings—all criminal trials must be fair and open. It protects the accused, or defendant, from government powers during a criminal proceeding. You also have the right to have legal representation protecting your rights and to cross-examine your accusers and witnesses against you.

The **Eighth Amendment** states that excessive bail shall not be required, nor excessive fines imposed, nor cruel and unusual punishment inflicted. Although this amendment prohibits excessive bail, this language is often open to interpretation, and often differs depending on the accused crime. Certain crimes like murder or rape may require that no bail is set, and the accused is remanded back to jail. Such a ruling must be reasonable, depending upon the circumstances set before the court and judge.

Cruel and unusual punishment is oftentimes open for debate, as the death penalty can be applied to capital cases. The death penalty has been an issue that has been debated, and contested from state to state, right up to the Supreme Court.

The criminal justice system is comprised of numerous agencies that work on both the state and federal levels. These different agencies are separate and unique, but are part of a complex and interconnected system. Each agency has its own set of goals, but all work towards the common goal of justice.

Criminal Justice Agencies

It would be impossible to list every individual agency within the criminal justice system; however, let's examine the various categories of these agencies and their roles.

The first group includes law enforcement and police. Again, we see law enforcement on both a state and federal level, including local or state police and federal agencies such as the FBI and DEA. The FBI and DEA belong to the Department of Justice, while FEMA and the U.S. Secret Service fall under the jurisdiction of the Department of Homeland Security. On the state level, it is not just the state police; it also includes conservation officers, environmental protection officers, and even parole officers. Local levels include law enforcement for towns and other municipalities.

Their roles are numerous, but mostly include keeping the peace by maintaining public order, apprehending offenders and violators who break laws, preventing crime through public awareness and educational programs, and providing social services that encompass other noncrime related matters.

The next agency level that takes part in the criminal justice system is the judicial branch, also known as the courts. There are many types of courts, including small claims court, civil court, bankruptcy court, and family court. The most common and recognizable is criminal court.

Courts are responsible for adjudicating each case, and as we've learned, due process plays a major role in American court proceedings. **Adjudication** is the process in which the courts determine if a defendant is guilty or not guilty. They must follow the rule of law and invoke fair procedures during this process. In addition, the courts impose sentencing, under the sentencing laws and guidelines, for offenders who are found guilty.

Our judicial system works as a **dual court system**, which means it separates state courts completely from national or federal courts. Each case is tried in its respective jurisdiction where laws were violated.

The last segment of the system falls under **corrections**. The correctional system is by far one of the oldest, and is also one of the most controversial and scrutinized. Corrections are used to punish offenders who break and violate the law. The correctional system takes on many forms, but we typically associate corrections with jails and prisons, which we'll explore in more detail later on in this chapter. The corrections system also consists of probation and parole. The purpose of corrections is a question that remains a topic of debate to this day—is it for punishment or rehabilitation? We'll look closer at different methods of correction, and their benefits and drawbacks, later on in this chapter.

LAW ENFORCEMENT

Let's now turn our focus to those who enforce the law on a daily basis—the police, which is the body that enforces societal law.

History and Organization

Law enforcement, as with most aspects of our laws, courts, and political structures, can be traced back to English tradition. One of the oldest systems, dating back to before the thirteenth century, was called frankpledge. **Frankpledge** is a system of ten household units (known as tithings) that work together to uphold the law and ensure each other's safety—and bring violators to court. The system also made all males above the age of 12 part of the tithings. When a crime was committed and a male became aware of it, he had a responsibility to inform the others (also known as a hue and cry) and to apprehend the offender. If the members failed to perform their duties, the tithing was fined.

The American system is largely based on the ideas of the founding father of policing, **Sir Robert Peel**, who in 1829 created the first London police force. In tribute, officers were called "bobbies" after him. Peel's philosophies now comprise much of modern policing today.

Peel had a four-part mandate. His goals were to do the following:

- Prevent crime without repressive force or use of the military
- Maintain public order by nonviolent means
- Reduce conflict between the police and public
- Show efficiency through the absence of crime

These mandates are still prevalent in today's policing.

American Policing—Historical Periods

American policing can be broken down into three historical periods.

The Political Era

The first period is the **Political Era**, which took place from 1840 to 1920. In this era, there were close ties between the police and political leaders. The police were loyal to the mayors and their parties—in other words, the police helped keep local politicians in power and the police were paid and received favors for their work and loyalty.

Corrupt politicians and their regimes used local police forces to harass and intimidate their political rivals. During this era, there was poor oversight and few regulations. This led to all sorts of corruption, which included discriminating against new immigrants and suppression of competing political parties.

Additionally, there were no standards or procedures to become a police officer, except for political connections, and for new officers training was limited. This bred more corruption. Newly appointed officers were often trained by veteran officers, who taught them all about the corrupt practices between the police, the community, and the politicians.

However, not everything in this era was bad or corrupt. As cities grew and with the influx of immigrants, police officers became extremely integrated within their communities. Officers were often seen as the only public servants on the street, and they took on a wide range of tasks that included community service—for instance, they served in soup kitchens, helped the homeless find shelter, and assisted immigrants in finding jobs.

In 1845, New York City created the first full-time paid police force. Because this era was filled with corruption, positions and ranks were paid off. For example, becoming a New York City police captain cost $10,000. Besides power, a lot of extra benefits and payoffs likely came along with that rank. However, this corrupt system couldn't last forever, and with the rise of reformers who wanted to change the relationship between the police and politicians, the second era of policing arose.

The Professional Model

The **Professional Model**, from 1920 through 1970, moved away from the corruption as the progressive movement began to influence policing. The progressives were largely made up of upper middle class and educated individuals. Some of their goals were to create a more efficient government and to have more services for the less fortunate in society. These reformers wanted the police and the police departments to become more professional.

August Vollmer, who was chief of police in Berkeley, California from 1909–1932, was one of the leading proponents of professional policing. He upgraded the police through technology, training, and even started a motorcycle unit.

In order for lasting change to happen, there were certain elements the reformers felt needed to be put in place:

- First, they wanted police to stay out of politics; they felt the police should be neutral when it came to political leaders. This is true today, as police departments do not endorse candidates for office.
- They wanted the police to be well trained. Training is a major component of professional policing. Training never ends for law enforcement—it is a constant reminder that as society becomes more complex, policing has to continually evolve to reflect the changing needs of society.
- They wanted assurance that all laws would be enforced equally.
- There was a great call for police departments to use new technology, including day-to-day and in training, as well. This continues today—as technology advances, law enforcement must constantly stay trained in the latest weapons, non-lethal weapons, and computers, among other new developments.
- Finally, the reformers requested that the main task of the police be to fight crime.

Community Policing

This progressive era then moved into the next one, known as **Community Policing**. In the early 1970s, policing moved away from traditional crime fighting and moved toward services to benefit the community. Police departments did not want to isolate the community and hoped for a better relationship between the community and the police. This is not to say that the police stopped enforcing the law—rather, they expanded their roles to include more social service calls.

Community policing calls for the police to build partnerships with the communities that they serve. This movement broadened the responsibilities of the police. As this era of community policing continues, some criminologists suggest that a new model of policing should be established. As a result of 9/11 and other terrorist attacks, the next suggested era might be labeled **Homeland Security**. Time will tell what the next official era and its components will be in this ever-changing world.

Structuring of Police Departments

The structure of modern day police departments can be traced back to Sir Robert Peel. During his construction of the London police force, he realized that the military could not police the streets and communities for numerous reasons. However, during the transition from a military force to a police force, Peele realized that even though the military could not effectively patrol the streets, the police department should model itself structurally like the military to be most effective. As a result of this, we often refer to the police as a paramilitary organization.

As in the military, police departments have hierarchies that resemble military ranks. There may be differences between the two institutions, but there is no doubt that there is rank structure within police departments. This hierarchy is also called a **chain of command**. The chain of command provides structure that defines ranks and authority over subordinates. This structure creates accountability, discipline, and control. Another term that may be used to describe police structure is **command and control**.

A common rank structure in policing (in order from lowest to highest ranked) is as follows:

Commander

⬆

Captain

⬆

Lieutenant

⬆

Sergeant

⬆

Detective

⬆

Police Officer

After the rank of captain, titles and structure may vary depending on the particular police department.

Some roles and functions of police in our society seem obvious—for instance, the protection of life and property. This is actually a simplistic view of the responsibilities that police take on. Police forces can and do have more of a personal role in modern society, and the community involvement portion of their jobs is often overlooked. Their service includes community outreach, such as speaking at schools and businesses and promoting educational programs such as D.A.R.E., a drug prevention and awareness program.

Other police-sponsored programs may include running a police athletic league; offering the chance to ride along with a local patrol officer; and hosting local parades, picnics, and holiday parties. Social media is a key tool for the police to get out their message and promote community relations.

Other responsibilities that fall under the purview of the police are investigating crimes, gathering information, interviewing victims and witnesses, testifying in court, and establishing crime scenes when necessary. Most of these functions, including traffic enforcement, fall under the routines of patrol. While performing patrol duties, police may also respond to emergencies such as car accidents and medical calls.

Along with patrol duties, an officer's duties include service calls. Up to 80 percent of all calls that an officer responds to may be service related. Some of these include the following:

- Searching for a lost child
- Medical calls
- Lost or abandoned pets
- Traffic control
- Assisting the homeless
- Civil matters such as landlord/tenant disputes

In addition to the everyday emergencies that police officers respond to when assisting the public, they also act as first responders. The police are often the first line of response to natural disasters and terrorist attacks, and lead rescue and recovery efforts for their communities.

As you can see, the roles and functions of law enforcement have become more complex over time. The age-old job of fighting and preventing crime will always be a cornerstone of police work, but the roles of the police will constantly change and evolve in response to the issues and demands of a changing society.

Societal needs are the driving force behind policing, and dictate police responses, attitudes, procedures, and changes in police culture. Let's examine some recent trends.

Antiterrorism has been an important issue, depending on the prevalence of national or local incidents. Police officers must stay vigilant to protect cities and communities from these acts, which goes hand-in-hand with the need for training and military-style equipment to combat and respond to such catastrophic incidents—even on the local level. These are necessities, but can often conflict with a society's perception of the police as too militant and aggressive. Police must work to balance this perception with the realities of their duty to protect.

Technology has most definitely shaped society's norms and behavior, and modern policing is no different. Of course, technology such as forensics and DNA have had a hugely beneficial impact on police and criminal investigations; however, there are other technological aspects that have also had an impact on policing.

Body cameras are another advancement that is gaining in popularity, and controversy. Pushback from police who are reluctant to wear them, differing opinions on when the cameras should be activated, and defining the legality of revealing recorded footage remain hot-button issues. As with anything else new to the technology field, procedures will continue to evolve.

Immigration is a particularly hot topic of conversation and controversy in today's society, and has ramifications for law enforcement as well. Issues facing police today include everything from learning how to work within communities that are non-English speaking to determining if an immigrant is legal or illegal and violated federal immigration laws. Also, cultural differences can make a simple police encounter more challenging because of potential differences in customs and traditions.

The use and perception of appropriate or excessive force by the police remains a hot-button issue. Close scrutiny by the public and media brings with it the possibility of civil unrest, as we have seen in many instances. This, in turn, potentially creates more distrust between the police and the community, and can erode the core of police community relations.

Occupational Characteristics

Police subculture contains many elements that make it unique. The first is called **working personality**, or the emotional and behavioral characteristics developed by members of a group in response to their work situation and environmental influences. The two main elements of working personality when it comes to police work are

1. Awareness of the threat of danger—learning to be suspicious of people and their behavior and always being on high alert.
2. The need to maintain personal authority. Police officers are constantly establishing their authority with the public, which at times affects their authority and power.

Another aspect of subculture can be found in **police morality**. Officers are placed in constant predicaments in which they must make quick decisions and determine right from wrong. As a result, police officers oftentimes develop a sense of high morality, which eases an officer's conscience during tense social interactions and dilemmas where they have to make quick and just decisions. A high morality also gives officers a sense of positivity about themselves as they work long hours and try to protect the public and keep communities safe.

Due to the nature of police work, it also creates a phenomenon called **police isolation**. Police isolation occurs when officers remove themselves from society, as they believe that the public is suspicious and hostile towards them. This is part of the subculture that currently exists in law enforcement. There are many reasons why this occurs, but one is that police often interact with society at the worst of times, like during crimes, injuries, and death, which can cause officers to pull away from society. Another isolating factor is the strange and long hours and irregular shifts within police culture.

Police isolation can lead officers to create more barriers with the public, as they naturally fall back within their own group or subculture. Officers often feel that the only people who truly understand them are other officers and family members. There are many types of stress that police officers face:

- **Work stress** that comes with law enforcement is part of the subculture that strengthens and increases internal police bonds. Law enforcement creates a large amount of stress that also results in high suicide rates, divorce, alcohol issues, and other related health conditions.
- **External stress** is produced by the threats and dangers of police work that officers may encounter on a regular basis.

- **Organizational stress** is created through the inner structure of police departments. Long hours, shift changes, and strict rules and procedures can contribute to this type of stress.
- **Personal stress** can occur when officers struggle to get along with peers and adjust their value systems.
- **Operational stress** results from dealing with the negative parts of society, which creates distrust in people whom officers encounter.

Now that you have a thorough overview of policing, let's turn our focus to the courts and how they operate.

THE COURT SYSTEM

This next section will detail the ins and outs of the U.S. court system—including its history, organization, and processes.

History of the Court System

Article III, Section 1 of the U.S. Constitution states:

"The judicial powers of the United States shall be vested in one Superior Court and in such inferior courts as the Congress may from time to time ordain and establish."

Passed in 1789, The Judiciary Act created provisions for the Supreme Court. It also established that the court would consist of a Chief Justice and five Associate Justices. **John Jay** was the first Justice appointed by George Washington.

The Supreme Court had no control over the cases that went before them until 1891. It was then that the Justices began reviewing cases through certiorari. **Certiorari**, in legal terms, means *to make sure*, as in an appeal. In other words, it is a written order from the higher court asking the lower court for the records of a case for review. Colonies also created functioning courts. This combination of courts by the early colonials, and the creation of the federal court system through the U.S. Constitution, was the beginning foundation of our court system.

Organization and Structure

As we discussed earlier, the United States operates under a dual court system, which in essence establishes a federal and state system, unlike other countries that have a singular national court system. Each level will hear and preside over cases that fall into their legal jurisdictions. Federal courts will deal with crimes violating federal laws like drug trafficking, counterfeiting, kidnapping, and terrorist activities to name a few. On the state level, each state enforces its state constitution and laws. The majority of cases that are heard before the courts fall under the state level, as they enforce many more laws, including misdemeanors and minor violations.

The federal court system is comprised of 94 judicial districts that cover all federal laws. The location of the crime committed determines which district court covers the case. Within these 94 district courts, there are 12 regional circuits, which cover the U.S. Court of Appeals. If you wanted to appeal your case, it would be heard in the corresponding court of appeals within that district.

In addition to the 12 circuits, there are two appellate courts in Washington, D.C. The U.S. Supreme Court is the highest court in the land. It focuses on constitutional issues on both a state and federal level.

The states are set up on a similar basis, with some differences. On a state level, cases start in a trial court to determine guilt or innocence. Depending on the type of crime committed, a case could wind up in a **court of limited jurisdiction**. This trial court handles only misdemeanors and civil lawsuits for small amounts of money, which varies from state to state. On a state level, there are also **courts of general jurisdiction**, which hear felony cases and civil lawsuits, and impose prison sentences. In some states, general jurisdiction courts will also hear all types of criminal cases and violations including traffic cases. The next level is a **court of appeals**. These appellate courts only review judicial errors from the lower courts, and do not determine guilt or innocence. The last level is known as **courts of last resorts**, which are for final appeal. Sometimes the courts of last resorts are also known as the state Supreme Court, the court of appeals, or high court.

Whether state or federal, both systems start at a trial level court and then proceed upwards to a court of appeals and then to the highest court.

The judicial system is not only split between a federal and state level, but also between an adult and juvenile system. Let's take a closer look.

Adult and Juvenile Court Systems

For starters, the terminology is different for adults. An adult who is accused is known as a **defendant**, the accusatory court document is known as a

complaint, and a hearing is called a **trial**. Trials in adult court are open to the public—you have a right to have a trial before your peers. During the trial, if one is found guilty he or she is sentenced with the main purpose of punishment in mind.

Juvenile courts, for the most part, completely differ from adult courts. However, there are some similarities, such as the right to an attorney, the right to cross-examine witnesses, protection from self-incrimination, notice of charges, and the need to be found guilty beyond a reasonable doubt. Let's look at some of the differences and how the juvenile system operates in contrast to the adult system.

In the juvenile system, the juvenile is referred to as the **minor**. Trial proceedings in juvenile court are called **adjudication hearings**, and the minor does not have the right to a public trial. Proceedings are behind closed doors to protect the minor's identity, and a judge will decide on guilt or innocence. There is no jury system because a juvenile's peers cannot judge him or her.

The ages for juvenile courts may vary from state to state, but can run between ages 10 to 16 and in some instances up to 18. However, juveniles may be tried as adults for serious violent offenses.

The juvenile courts do not use the terms *crimes* or *criminal acts*; they use **delinquent acts**. The courts are more lenient when it comes to the admissibility of evidence, and sentencing hearings are called **disposition hearings**. Once someone is found guilty, the purpose of the court is to keep the minor's best interests in mind and to seek rehabilitation—not punishment. The judges often use diversionary programs like probation, counseling, community service, and restitution.

Pretrial, Trial, and Post-Trial Processes

The criminal justice system is set in motion when a crime has been committed and the police begin an investigation. Following an arrest, the due process clause is attached to the offender as he or she moves through the court system.

As a case proceeds, the district attorney or prosecutor is in charge. During this pretrial phase, the prosecutor implements their policies when reviewing each case to help guide them in making legal decisions. These decisions can be seen in three phases. They are:

- **Legal sufficiency:** The prosecutor reviews the case and arrest to ensure that it meets the legal standard to pursue and move forward.
- **System efficiency:** Here, the prosecutor establishes policies to engage in speedy and early disposition of cases. Cases are screened, and some cases are plea bargained in exchange for a quick guilty plea to expedite the flow of cases.
- **Trial sufficiency:** The prosecutor determines if the case is strong enough and meets the legal standards to prosecute at trial and obtain a conviction. They review the police work, victims, and witnesses in order to proceed with a trial.

Prior to any trial, there are numerous steps that take place to protect the rights of the defendant and to determine if probable cause exists. This process works to ensure that the offender's constitutional rights are protected.

The first step in the process is the **initial appearance**. Initial appearance is when the offender is brought before the judge, within a reasonable amount of time, to be given formal notice of charges and information about their rights. At this point, the judge reviews the evidence to decide if the case can move forward. A bail hearing also takes place during this appearance. **Bail** is defined as a specific amount of money set by a judge to be paid as a condition of pretrial release to make sure that the accused will return to court.

The next step, especially for serious crimes, is a **preliminary hearing** with a judge, or a **grand jury** in front of a special jury. This process determines whether there is probable cause that a crime was committed and that the accused person committed it. This step does not determine guilt or innocence, but rather examines the legal standard of probable cause.

Once a judge or grand jury determines probable cause, the accused is processed to the next phase—arraignment. **Arraignment** takes place when the accused appears in court to hear the indictment or information that was produced in the previous phase. In other words, if probable cause was found against an individual, a document has to be produced by the prosecutor and filed in court. This is again for the accused to know what charges were filed against him or her in a preliminary hearing or grand jury. In a preliminary hearing, it is called an **information**, while a grand jury produces an **indictment**.

This sets the stage for the pretrial process. One of the many phases of the pretrial process is what is known as discovery. **Discovery** is the exchange of information between the prosecutor and the defense. The responsibility falls upon the prosecutor to relinquish evidence to the defense, to ensure both sides are on a level playing field during the trial. The prosecutor cannot surprise the defense at the last minute. This gives the defense adequate time to prepare a legal defense, once they receive the prosecutorial information through discovery.

Another pretrial step that takes place is known as a motion. A **motion** is basically a request to the court to do something or take action. There are all types of motions filed in a criminal case. One is a **motion to dismiss**, which is made if the defense feels an indictment or information has been completed incorrectly, or some sort of judicial error was made. This motion states that in the name of fundamental fairness, the court should dismiss the charges.

Another common form of motion is a **motion to suppress**. If the defense feels that any of the evidence in a case was obtained illegally under the Fourth Amendment, a motion will be filed before the court. The defendant will be allowed to testify before the judge. Based on the evidence, he or she will make a ruling about the admissibility of the evidence. Some of the evidence may be admissible and some of it may not be—the judge will determine this on a case-by-case basis.

The defense may also file a motion for a **change of venue**, which is where the trial will take place. If the defense feels they cannot get a fair trial at the jurisdiction where the crime occurred, the motion will be filed to request a new location. Factors that come into play when requesting a new venue include media coverage, community involvement, and any other public negativity surrounding the case. The judge will determine if the defendant can get a fair trial in the original jurisdiction.

In the beginning phase of the trial, a process takes place called a **voir dire**, which is the process of selecting a jury. This is where the prosecution and defense question prospective jurors and determine who will sit as jurors and alternates. The selection process also involves **peremptory challenge**, where each party is allowed a number of objections, without reason, to eliminate potential jurors.

Once the voir dire is completed and the jury is set, the trial will begin and the judge will give preliminary instructions to the jury. The judge will explain obligations, the law, and the presumption of innocence to the jury. **Opening statements** by both the prosecutor and defense then follow, which give both parties an opportunity to address the jury and explain the facts of the case.

The trial process in the United States is an **adversarial system**, wherein both parties argue for their side. After both parties present their cases and witnesses, the prosecutor can call rebuttal witnesses to disprove the defense, and then the defense is allowed to rebut the prosecutor's evidence.

The trial then progresses to the final stages, with **closing arguments** delivered by both sides. The attorneys address the jury once more, and present them with the facts of the case and the law. This gives both parties the opportunity to summarize their cases. When arguments are completed, the judge will give the jury final instructions on the law, the burden of proof, and the elements of the crime they're judging.

Then, the jury will be removed from the courtroom and begin their deliberations in an effort to reach a verdict. During deliberations, the jury has no contact with the outside world. When the jury has reached a verdict of guilt or innocence, they will return to court to read the verdict to the defendant. If the verdict is not guilty and the defendant is acquitted, the case is over and the accused is free to go. However, if the jury finds the defendant guilty then the sentencing phase is next.

Sentencing Issues and Trends

After a guilty verdict, the judge will determine a sentencing date. The date will be set some time in the future, in order to create a **Pre-Sentence Investigation Report (PSI)**. This report, led by the probation department, is created after interviewing the defendant and conducting an investigation of the defendant's past history, which includes criminal history, family, medical issues, and employment. The defendant is permitted to make a statement in the report, as well. Once all relevant background information is complete, a sentence recommendation will be given to the judge.

During the sentencing hearing, the judge will review the PSI and conduct a hearing to determine the sentence. Witnesses may be called, and both the defendant and victim can make statements. The **victim impact statement** allows the victim or family members to address the court, either in a written or verbal statement. The judge will then, under the sentencing guidelines, hand the defendant the appropriate sentence.

More than 2 million people are currently incarcerated in the U.S. prison system. This high number stems from the elevated levels of drug offenses and the consequences of the "get tough on crime" policies of the 1980s and 1990s. Currently, the federal prison population is growing, and half of the prison population is there for drug-related offenses.

Current sentencing trends have included some states abolishing mandatory penalties for drug offenses. More and more, courts are turning to alternative sentencing programs including community supervision, shock probation, drug courts, and treatment programs. Society is always looking for alternative methods for punishment and rehabilitation, as prison sentences can be very costly.

You should now have a solid overview of the courts and how they operate within the criminal justice system. Let's now turn our focus to corrections.

CORRECTIONS

This section covers all aspects of corrections: its history, the different systems used, and its evolution in a changing society.

History of Corrections

The American system of corrections, like other aspects of its criminal justice system, was derived from the English during the colonial period (1620–1776). In 1682, William Penn, the founder of Pennsylvania, adopted what was known as **The Great Law**, which was based on humane Quaker principles and emphasized hard labor in a house of corrections as punishment. Eventually, the colonies moved away from The Great Law, and jail time gave way to harsh physical punishments including whippings, branding, and mutilation.

After the American Revolution, theories regarding criminal punishment took another turn. The new theory of corrections believed that offenders could be reformed, which gave way to the birth of the **penitentiary**. Offenders were sent to penitentiaries for isolation from society, in order to reflect on their past behaviors, and hopefully to repent.

Pennsylvania opened the first penitentiary in 1790, based on the concept of **solitary confinement**. In 1819, New York was soon to follow with its first penitentiary located in Auburn. Here, inmates were held in isolation at night and worked with each other in complete silence during the day. They were issued prison striped uniforms.

In the 1800s, the **Reformatory Movement** emerged, and in 1876, Elmira, New York was home to the first reformatory prison. The Reformatory Movement emphasized training for prisoners, who were treated for what were perceived to be the social, biological, and psychological root causes of deviant behavior. Prisoners followed strict schedules that included work, academics, and vocational training.

There have always been debates about corrections and its role and purpose in society. Over time, corrections and its methods have changed according to society's needs and beliefs, but the main concept has never wavered—to protect society. Essentially, the system wants people to behave and conform to society's rules, laws, and norms, and criminal behavior is punished.

Purpose

The U.S. correctional system carries with it four goals:

- The first is **retribution**, which we covered earlier. This refers to the "eye for an eye" philosophy and calls for a deserved punishment that fits the crime.
- The second is **deterrence**, which is based on the belief that people's behavior can be controlled by the notion that criminal behavior will result in punishment. There are two types of deterrence: general deterrence, which is intended for society as a whole to prevent criminal behavior, and specific deterrence, which is targeted toward offenders with the hope that they will not commit any further criminal behavior.
- Next is **incapacitation**—the assumption that society can be protected from offenders by placing them in a correctional facility for a length of time. Execution falls under this umbrella, as well.
- Finally, **rehabilitation** is based on the notion of changing or restoring the offender to alter his future behavior and reform him as he returns to society. This is accomplished through education and vocational training.

The courts and correctional system have developed various forms of punishment and sentencing to fit the needs of society and the criminal justice system. With recent issues of prison overcrowding and a lack of resources for probationary services, counties and states have needed to make some changes to their sentencing guidelines and structures.

One of these changes is called **intermediate sanctions**, which are punishments that are not as severe or costly as prison sentences, but are more restrictive than regular or traditional probation. These sanctions can include monetary fines or forfeiture of illegally gained assets. They can also restrict one's freedom through home confinement, strict probation supervision, and community service. These sanctions are more effective when they are used in combination with each other. Additionally, these sanctions take into account the type of offense committed, the traits and attributes of the offender, and how best to serve the community.

Juvenile Correctional System

The regular adult prison system is relatively simple compared to the juvenile system. Adult prisons are intended for individuals 18 years and older and have fewer rehabilitative services than juvenile facilities. (Even though the juvenile system has more services than the adult system, there are more adult facilities in the form of jails and prisons.)

The juvenile correctional system contains many different correctional alternatives for the juvenile offender. As opposed to adult corrections, where the goal is punishment, the goal of the juvenile system is **rehabilitation**. Because of this goal, and the fact that the juvenile system has fewer institutional facilities, one alternative is juvenile probation. During probation, juveniles are closely supervised by probation officers and must follow strict rules and conditions, which are set by the juvenile court. These include drug-treatment programs and group counseling facilities. For these **community treatment alternatives**, the assumption is that the offender is not a danger to the community and will likely rehabilitate.

The juvenile system also contains **residential community treatment**. In residential treatment, a juvenile is placed in a nonsecure facility that is closely monitored by trained members. These treatment programs are composed in several different ways:

- **Group homes** are residences that are supervised by trained counselors who provide counseling, education, job training, and family living. The number of juveniles usually ranges from 12 to 15.
- **Foster care** is for juveniles who are orphans, or whose parents cannot provide care for them. The juvenile is placed in foster care with families to care and provide for them, with the intention of returning them to the community.
- **Family group homes** are simply a combination of group homes and foster care.
- **Rural programs** give juveniles the opportunity to work at forestry camps, ranches, and farms.

Other probationary programs include **Juvenile Intensive Probation Supervision (JIPS)**, which is an alternative to incarceration. In JIPS, the juvenile is assigned to a probation officer with a very small caseload. These juveniles fall into a high-risk category and therefore receive close daily supervision by probation officers.

In **electronic monitoring**, another form of probation, the juvenile wears an electronic device and is monitored by the probation department. Movements are monitored, and limited to school, programs, court, and work, while the rest of the time is spent at home. Random visits and phone calls also ensure that the juvenile is home at appropriate times.

Capital Punishment

Let's now turn our focus to a discussion of capital punishment.

Capital punishment has almost always been a part of correctional history. It continues to be one of the most controversial topics in the criminal justice system. Capital punishment in the United States is still used and has been involved in many court cases, including cases adjudicated by the Supreme Court. Cases involving the death penalty often raise constitutional issues involving the Eighth Amendment, which forbids cruel and unusual punishment, as well as the Fourteenth Amendment clause of providing equality in justice.

The death penalty is used in federal, state, and military courts. Each state has the option of implementing the death penalty in its sentencing laws. As mentioned, the death penalty has been challenged many times based on its merits and constitutionality. Under the Eighth Amendment, the death penalty has been tested—not only with regard to execution of the offender, but also regarding different methods of execution.

A challenge that the U.S. Supreme Court faced in the past was based on lethal injection, particularly that lethal injections violated the Eighth Amendment. In 2008, the Supreme Court denied this claim and stated that lethal injection was not a violation of the Eighth Amendment.

One of the most famous cases involving capital punishment was *Furman v. Georgia*, in 1972. The Civil Rights movement had raised concerns about the death penalty—not only with regard to race, but also with regard to how the sentence was imposed. In this case, the U.S. Supreme Court banned the use of capital punishment. This case did not rule on the death penalty with regard to the Eighth Amendment, but rather from the standpoint of how it was applied to defendants. The Supreme Court determined that when courts applied the death penalty it was arbitrary and capricious, meaning there were no set laws or guidelines. There was no system in place, and sentencing was based on prosecutorial discretion, leading to a lot of disparity and questions of racial bias. In other words, the death penalty was chosen randomly as to when and to whom it was applied.

Following the Furman case, states that wanted to use the death penalty as a punishment needed to meet the Supreme Court criteria. These states implemented uniformity in death penalty cases for first-degree murder with aggravating circumstances.

Prison Organization

Let's review common terminology regarding incarceration.

Jails and **prisons** are probably the most misused terms in the correctional and criminal justice system. Like everything else in this system, these institutions are organized and structured. The first level of organization is **police booking** or holding cells, the first places offenders will pass through. Police use these facilities to detain offenders while they are being processed. Offenders will eventually be transported to larger facilities.

The next level is **jails**. Jails are used for multiple purposes. The primary purpose of jails is to hold defendants awaiting trial or who could not make bail. Also, if offenders are convicted of misdemeanor crimes, they would serve their time in local jails. Jails will also hold inmates for federal and state crimes who are waiting to be transported to the proper jurisdiction. Individuals with mental illnesses who are waiting to be transferred to a proper medical facility will also be housed in jails. The majority of inmates found in jails have not been convicted of any crimes, with the exception of misdemeanor offenses. Instead, these inmates are for the most part waiting to be charged, tried, or sentenced and transported to a proper facility or jurisdiction.

There are a few different types of jails. **Municipal jails** can be found in large cities like Los Angles and New York City, which are homes to the two largest city jails in the country. **County jails** are more common, in which the county will house and supervise the correctional facility located within its borders.

State prisons are correctional institutions that are used only for convicted offenders who are found guilty of felony crimes. Inmates who are sent to prison have been sentenced by the courts to serve a term of more than a year. State prisons can be broken down into certain categories, including male-only, female-only, and those for youth offenders convicted of serious crimes.

Prisons are also classified by the offense committed and the type of security provided:

- In **maximum security prisons**, the facility emphasizes security, with armed guards, towers, and restricted inmate movement. Here, there are fewer vocational and educational programs for rehabilitation.
- In a **medium security prison**, there is still a strong emphasis on security, but also opportunities for education, counseling, and other rehabilitation programs.
- Inmates in **minimum security prisons** may work in unsupervised locations outside the facility, such as prison farms, or take part in other rehabilitative programs, such as vocational and educational programs.

Federal prisons are used for all federal crimes, and are operated by the Bureau of Prisons. There are currently more than 100 federal correctional facilities, which are classified like state institutions into minimum, medium, and maximum security prisons.

Inmate Characteristics

Let's go over some facts about the current prison population in the United States:

- Presently, the prison population is approximately 92 percent male and 8 percent female.
- Approximately 26 percent of inmates are in the 20–29 age range, 31 percent are in the 30–39 age range, 23 percent are in the 40–49 age range, and 13 percent are in the 50–59 age range.
- African Americans make up 37 percent of the prison population, whites make up 32 percent, and Hispanics make up 22 percent.

Prison life poses many challenges for inmates, and subcultures within the system have a deep effect on their personalities, both during and after incarceration.

Prisoner violence, used for intimidation, power, and status, is common among inmates. Prison gangs are typically based on racial or ethnic backgrounds, and provide inmates with protection and a sense of belonging. Gangs create an atmosphere of violence and fear that can be found across many prison populations.

Along with inmate violence, which can shape people's attitudes and characteristics, sexual violence has an unfortunate presence in prison life. As a result of the prevalence of violent sexual acts in prison, the **Prison Rape Elimination Act** was signed into law in 2003. This law was designed to prevent violent sexual assaults among prisoners. However, because victim reporting of these assaults is sparse, it has been difficult to obtain accurate numbers, implement proper protections, and determine the law's effectiveness.

Issues and Trends

These issues and many more, including the accelerated decline in physical and mental health that takes place in correctional facilities, can cause extreme stress, depression, and other negative effects in inmates.

As mentioned previously, the correctional system and the pieces that comprise it are constantly changing. As new public policies develop, government officials must invest in correctional facilities to keep their communities safe. However, rising costs and the rampant issue of prison overcrowding may necessitate alternative methods for sentencing offenders. For example, in the juvenile system, the trend toward developing community-based residential facilities, rather than incarceration, continues to grow.

Another trend within correctional institutions is an ever-increasing influx of women (currently, the majority of incarcerated women are between the ages of 24 and 45, and half have racial or ethnic minority backgrounds). Approximately one-third of incarcerated women have been convicted of violent crimes.

As a result, corrections officials are now facing a new set of issues and challenges. Different facilities are needed for female inmates, with distinct programs to fulfill their needs. One of the most important issues female inmates face is childcare. Children who were cared for by a single-parent mother who is incarcerated are usually placed with relatives, friends, or in state foster care. Female inmates who are pregnant while incarcerated can be a challenge for institutions. Prisons are not traditionally structured for childcare, and the birth of a child by a female inmate raises many issues of concern. Typically, most states do not have family programs or facilities to keep the mother and child together. The average time that a female inmate spends with her newborn is three weeks, at which time the child is removed and placed with family members or social services.

Another trend in the correctional system over the last couple of decades has been the rise and popularity of private prisons—facilities that look similar to government-run prisons, but are operated by private, for-profit companies. These prisons house inmates from local, state, and federal governments for a fee. A private facility will charge, on average, $25 to $100 per day per inmate.

Prison privatization comes with many controversies. Advocates for privatization argue that it can reduce jail overcrowding, reduce staff costs, and save local and federal governments money. Supporters of these programs also claim that they can run these facilities more cheaply and efficiently than the states or federal government.

However, in order for private prisons to survive and make a profit, they must fill the facility with inmates and keep staffing and rehabilitative program costs down. Research has shown privately run prisons may not be that cost-effective or beneficial at all—both for inmates and for the criminal justice system. The debate on privatization will continue.

SUMMING IT UP

- A crime is an act committed in violation of established law. There are two types of crime: the first is **mala in se**, which are offenses that are immoral and considered wrong, like murder, rape, robbery, and assault. **Mala prohibita** crimes are offenses that are not necessarily inherently wrong, but are prohibited by law, such as gambling, prostitution, drug use, or traffic violations.
- U.S. crime is reported and tracked by the **Uniform Crime Reporting Program**, which establishes patterns and trends and breaks down crime by location, demographics, and other statistics.
- The **classical criminology** theory views criminal behavior as a conscious choice, which can be deterred by establishing predictable punishments. It also prioritizes quick punishment over severe punishment, and calls for humane prison systems as well.
- In the **utilitarian** philosophy of crime, philosophers believe that whether actions are morally right or morally wrong depends on the effects and results of the action, and that people will avoid crime to avoid pain and unpleasant consequences.
- The **positivist theory of criminology** suggests that crime is a result of an individual's sociological, biological, and psychological factors, and that the punishment should be tailored to fit the crime, rather than having a nonspecific set of general consequences for breaking the law. This view of criminality was supported further by psychologist William Sheldon's biological classification systems, psychologist Sigmund Freud's theory that a person's personality and behavior are controlled by early childhood influences, and Edwin Sutherland's sociological theory that criminal behavior comes from a person's personal influences in life.
- Other crime theories include the **control theory**, in which criminal behavior is caused by weakened social ties; the **labeling theory**, in which crime is a social construct instead of an individual act; and **anomie**, in which crime is a result of a breakdown in social rules and norms.
- The types of crime include **felonies** (major crimes punishable by incarceration for at least a year, and up to the death penalty), **misdemeanors** (minor crimes punishable by incarceration for a year or less), **visible crime** (street crime), **occupational crime** (crime of opportunity, like stealing from an employer), **organized crime** (criminal acts related to gambling, drugs, and prostitution committed by groups like drug cartels, the Mafia, etc.), **crimes without victims** (exchanges of illegal goods or services), **political crimes** (terrorist acts or crimes against the state), and **cybercrime** (crimes committed using computers or digital means).

- In crime reporting, the **dark figure of crime** is the difference between reported crimes and unreported crimes. It affects overall crime and reporting statistics. The FBI attempts to assess the dark figure of crime by conducting the annual National Crime Victimization Survey (NCVS) to determine the gap between reported **index crimes** (such as murder, arson, burglary, rape, and felony assaults) and crimes that go unreported.

- Factors that affect **juvenile delinquency** (criminal behavior by minors) include drug use, gang activity, and lack of economic or social resources. Gang activity in particular has increased, and includes more members from different age groups and different genders.

- The concept of codified laws goes back to the Hammurabi code, which was formed in 1750 B.C.E. Babylon and established the idea of punishing crimes. The code, which was based on the concept of "an eye for an eye," was the first to set legal standards for all forms of societal behavior, with varying penalties for crimes ranging from financial consequences to the death penalty.

- The American justice system developed out of the concept of English common law, and was refined and shaped by William Penn after the Revolutionary War. The U.S. Constitution further defined equal rights and legal protections for citizens.

- Due process, or fair treatment in all legal matters, is a fundamental concept of the American justice system. The Fifth Amendment to the Constitution outlines due process for American citizens, stating that no citizen will be deprived of life, liberty, or property without notice, or a chance to defend in court. Due process was applied to all states as well in the Fourteenth Amendment.

- The criminal justice system is made up of three main segments: law enforcement, the courts, and corrections. Law enforcement agencies include police on the state and local level as well as federal agencies under the jurisdictions of the Department of Justice and the Department of Homeland Security. The judicial branch includes all types of courts, including criminal, civil, small claims, bankruptcy, and family courts. The judicial branch functions as a **dual court system**, separating federal courts from state courts. The corrections system includes prisons, as well as probation and parole programs.

- In the **Political Era** of American policing (1840–1920), there were close relationships between police and political leaders in which both parties traded favors in exchange for loyalty.

- In the **Professional Model** era (1920–1970), a more progressive version of policing was meant to create more efficient local government and more resources for less fortunate people. To achieve these goals, the reformers tried to separate policing and politics, emphasized constant training for police professionals, and emphasized that laws should be enforced equally.

- In the **Community Policing** era (1970–present), policing moved away from direct crime fighting and closer to developing relationships between communities and the police as a way of increasing social service and reducing crime.
- A police **chain of command** is a structure that defines ranks and authority for all members of the department. The highest ranks are typically Commander, then Captain, then Lieutenant, then Sergeant, then Detective, then Police Officer, though this can vary depending on the police department. Line function officers are out in the field, while staff function officers typically work within the police department itself (such as clerks and administrative staff).
- As policing needs grow and change with society, the nature of policing has evolved as well. Antiterrorism has become a major focus of American police work. Advancements in technology (like sophisticated forensics, DNA, and body cameras) have also affected how police officers work and function in their communities. Immigration violations and excessive force are also current hot-button topics being debated when it comes to modern policing.
- **Subculture** is important to police work, because the police community is often closed and separate from most of society. Police subculture is often defined by the following characteristics: **working personality** (the characteristics developed by a group in response to their work and environment), **police morality** (relying on conscience to solve problems), and **police isolation** (working apart from society due to perceived hostility toward police).
- Although juvenile and adult courts have different terminology and are handled separately, both follow the same general trial processes. After a defendant or minor has been charged, the prosecutor determines whether there is sufficient evidence for a trial. Once a formal charge is made, a defendant has the option to make bail before the trial, and may be entitled to a preliminary hearing with a judge or grand jury to determine probable cause. Attorneys for both sides work on **discovery** and **motions** for court actions before the trial starts. After jury selection, the trial begins, and both the defense attorney and the prosecutor present evidence to the judge and jury. Once both attorneys give closing arguments for their respective cases, the jury deliberates and arrives at a verdict.
- After a guilty verdict, a defendant's sentence is determined separately. A **Pre-Sentence Investigation Report (PSI)** is compiled, taking factors into account like the defendant's history and circumstances, as well as statements from victims of the crime.
- The U.S. corrections system originated in England's common law, and has developed punishment and sentencing to support a set of four goals: **retribution** (punishment for crime), **deterrence** (discouraging future crime),

incapacitation (taking offenders out of society), and **rehabilitation** (changing behavior). The juvenile prison system tends to focus on rehabilitation and alternative punishment and treatment programs that allow juveniles to re-enter society.

- **Capital punishment**, or the death penalty, is used in federal, state, and military courts, and can be implemented in laws at the state level. Capital punishment remains controversial due to constitutional debates over the cruel and unusual punishment outlined in the Eighth Amendment, as well as the Fourteenth Amendment clause ensuring justice applied equally.

- **Jails** are temporary holding facilities for defendants awaiting trial or hearings, defendants who could not make bail, or defendants serving misdemeanor sentences. **Prisons** are long-term correctional institutions that hold people convicted of felony crimes. Prisons are often divided by security level (maximum, medium, and minimum) or by demographic category (men's, women's, juvenile). **Federal prisons** hold people convicted of federal crimes.

Chapter 4

Criminal Justice Post-Test

POST-TEST ANSWER SHEET

1. Ⓐ Ⓑ Ⓒ Ⓓ
2. Ⓐ Ⓑ Ⓒ Ⓓ
3. Ⓐ Ⓑ Ⓒ Ⓓ
4. Ⓐ Ⓑ Ⓒ Ⓓ
5. Ⓐ Ⓑ Ⓒ Ⓓ
6. Ⓐ Ⓑ Ⓒ Ⓓ
7. Ⓐ Ⓑ Ⓒ Ⓓ
8. Ⓐ Ⓑ Ⓒ Ⓓ
9. Ⓐ Ⓑ Ⓒ Ⓓ
10. Ⓐ Ⓑ Ⓒ Ⓓ
11. Ⓐ Ⓑ Ⓒ Ⓓ
12. Ⓐ Ⓑ Ⓒ Ⓓ
13. Ⓐ Ⓑ Ⓒ Ⓓ
14. Ⓐ Ⓑ Ⓒ Ⓓ
15. Ⓐ Ⓑ Ⓒ Ⓓ
16. Ⓐ Ⓑ Ⓒ Ⓓ
17. Ⓐ Ⓑ Ⓒ Ⓓ

18. Ⓐ Ⓑ Ⓒ Ⓓ
19. Ⓐ Ⓑ Ⓒ Ⓓ
20. Ⓐ Ⓑ Ⓒ Ⓓ
21. Ⓐ Ⓑ Ⓒ Ⓓ
22. Ⓐ Ⓑ Ⓒ Ⓓ
23. Ⓐ Ⓑ Ⓒ Ⓓ
24. Ⓐ Ⓑ Ⓒ Ⓓ
25. Ⓐ Ⓑ Ⓒ Ⓓ
26. Ⓐ Ⓑ Ⓒ Ⓓ
27. Ⓐ Ⓑ Ⓒ Ⓓ
28. Ⓐ Ⓑ Ⓒ Ⓓ
29. Ⓐ Ⓑ Ⓒ Ⓓ
30. Ⓐ Ⓑ Ⓒ Ⓓ
31. Ⓐ Ⓑ Ⓒ Ⓓ
32. Ⓐ Ⓑ Ⓒ Ⓓ
33. Ⓐ Ⓑ Ⓒ Ⓓ
34. Ⓐ Ⓑ Ⓒ Ⓓ

35. Ⓐ Ⓑ Ⓒ Ⓓ
36. Ⓐ Ⓑ Ⓒ Ⓓ
37. Ⓐ Ⓑ Ⓒ Ⓓ
38. Ⓐ Ⓑ Ⓒ Ⓓ
39. Ⓐ Ⓑ Ⓒ Ⓓ
40. Ⓐ Ⓑ Ⓒ Ⓓ
41. Ⓐ Ⓑ Ⓒ Ⓓ
42. Ⓐ Ⓑ Ⓒ Ⓓ
43. Ⓐ Ⓑ Ⓒ Ⓓ
44. Ⓐ Ⓑ Ⓒ Ⓓ
45. Ⓐ Ⓑ Ⓒ Ⓓ
46. Ⓐ Ⓑ Ⓒ Ⓓ
47. Ⓐ Ⓑ Ⓒ Ⓓ
48. Ⓐ Ⓑ Ⓒ Ⓓ
49. Ⓐ Ⓑ Ⓒ Ⓓ
50. Ⓐ Ⓑ Ⓒ Ⓓ
51. Ⓐ Ⓑ Ⓒ Ⓓ

52. Ⓐ Ⓑ Ⓒ Ⓓ   **55.** Ⓐ Ⓑ Ⓒ Ⓓ   **58.** Ⓐ Ⓑ Ⓒ Ⓓ

53. Ⓐ Ⓑ Ⓒ Ⓓ   **56.** Ⓐ Ⓑ Ⓒ Ⓓ   **59.** Ⓐ Ⓑ Ⓒ Ⓓ

54. Ⓐ Ⓑ Ⓒ Ⓓ   **57.** Ⓐ Ⓑ Ⓒ Ⓓ   **60.** Ⓐ Ⓑ Ⓒ Ⓓ

CRIMINAL JUSTICE POST-TEST

Directions: Carefully read each of the following 60 questions. Choose the best answer to each question and fill in the corresponding circle on the answer sheet. The Answer Key and Explanations can be found following this post-test.

1. The majority of violent crimes that take place between an offender and a victim are

   A. interracial.
   B. biracial.
   C. unrelated to race.
   D. intraracial.

2. Crimes that are considered not necessarily wrong in and of themselves but are prohibited by law, such as drug offenses or prostitution, are called

   A. mala in se.
   B. mala prohibita.
   C. violations.
   D. morality crimes.

3. The criminologist who wrote *An Essay on Crimes and Punishments* and was a proponent of the classical criminology theory was

   A. Sigmund Freud.
   B. Edwin Sutherland.
   C. Cesare Lombroso.
   D. Cesare Beccaria.

4. The idea that criminal behavior stems from mental illness is known as

   A. XYY chromosome theory.
   B. labeling theory.
   C. psychological explanation.
   D. violent crime.

5. The theory that criminality stems from the broken ties between an individual and society is

A. classical criminology.
B. differential association.
C. control theory.
D. political crime.

6. Crimes that are committed from legal opportunities or businesses are called

A. felonies.
B. political crimes.
C. organized crimes.
D. occupational crimes.

7. Crimes that are considered street crimes and are most upsetting to the public are

A. visible crimes.
B. cybercrimes.
C. white-collar crimes.
D. misdemeanors.

8. The idea that some crimes occur and are never reported to the police is called

A. UCR.
B. crimes without victims.
C. juvenile delinquency.
D. the dark figure of crime.

9. An individual who has committed a criminal offense and falls under a particular age is known as a

A. neglected child.
B. dependent child.
C. juvenile delinquent.
D. recidivist.

10. One of the earliest criminal justice laws named after a ruler who dates back to Babylonian times (1750 B.C.E.) is known as

   A. Confucius' rules.
   B. Hammurabi code.
   C. Caesar's laws.
   D. Attila the Hun's laws.

11. Which term represents the theory of an "eye for an eye"?

   A. Restitution
   B. Due process
   C. Lex talionis
   D. Rehabilitation

12. The process that is founded on fair treatment in all legal matters and protects the rights of defendants, and also limits the powers of state and federal governments is called

   A. legislative process.
   B. equal protection.
   C. exclusionary rule.
   D. due process.

13. The double jeopardy clause states that

   A. people have the right to feel secure in their persons and houses.
   B. excessive bail is prohibited.
   C. a person cannot be subjected to prosecution more than once for the same offense in the same jurisdiction.
   D. individuals have the right to have legal representation.

14. The Fruit of the Poisonous Tree Doctrine can be found under which amendment?

   A. Second Amendment
   B. Fifth Amendment
   C. Fourth Amendment
   D. Fourteenth Amendment

15. Which amendment ensures an individual's protection from unreasonable searches and seizures from government agencies?

A. Fourth Amendment
B. Fourteenth Amendment
C. Sixth Amendment
D. Eighth Amendment

16. The Fourteenth Amendment states that

A. the prosecution needs to establish mens rea.
B. individuals are protected from self-incrimination.
C. no warrants will be issued without probable cause.
D. the due process clause is now binding to all the states.

17. When evidence is obtained from an illegal search and is not admissible in court, it is called

A. adjudication.
B. probable cause.
C. the exclusionary rule.
D. double jeopardy.

18. The agency within the criminal justice system that keeps the peace, maintains public order, and provides social services is

A. victim services.
B. the court system.
C. corrections.
D. law enforcement.

19. The agency within the criminal justice system that is the oldest segment in history and has the responsibility of punishment as well as rehabilitation is

A. law enforcement.
B. the judicial branch.
C. family court.
D. the correctional system.

20. Adjudication is the process that includes

A. the standard to make an arrest.
B. the standard to convict an individual in court.
C. the process in which the courts determine guilt or innocence.
D. the standard to determine a guilty state of mind.

21. The court system that the United States has is a

    A. one court system.
    B. Supreme Court.
    C. triple court system.
    D. dual court system.

22. Parole and probation fall under which system?

    A. The court system
    B. The correctional system
    C. Law enforcement
    D. They have their own separate systems.

23. Agencies such as the FBI and DEA are part of what system?

    A. Jurisdiction of courts
    B. Correctional agencies
    C. Law enforcement
    D. They are separate agencies unto themselves.

24. The status of the death penalty has been argued many times and has had many different outcomes in favor of it and against it. The debate of capital cases that have the death penalty as a punishment falls under which amendment?

    A. Eighth Amendment
    B. Fifth Amendment
    C. Fourth Amendment
    D. Sixth Amendment

25. Policing in America was based on what country's traditions?

    A. French
    B. Native American
    C. Canadian
    D. English

26. Sir Robert Peel created the first police force in London and had a four-part mandate that included

    A. creating a militia to maintain order.
    B. keeping the police and the community away from each other.
    C. reducing conflict between the police and the public.
    D. using as much force as possible to keep public order.

27. Policing can be broken down into different eras. Which era involved close ties and relationships between the police and political leaders?

A. The Community Policing Era
B. The Political Era
C. The Professional Era
D. The Crime Control Era

28. Which era was influenced by the Progressive movement, in which the reformers wanted the police to be well-trained and stay out of politics?

A. Community Policing Era
B. Political Era
C. The 9/11 Era
D. Professional Era

29. Police departments, like the military, have a hierarchy with ranks and a structure. That structure is called

A. chain of command.
B. management structure.
C. mid-management supervision.
D. rank organization.

30. The police serve the public and communities in many ways, including through sponsored police programs. An example of such a program is

A. sharing investigative techniques with the public.
B. assisting the police with traffic enforcement.
C. D.A.R.E.
D. having the police stay out of school activities and just leaving them to school officials.

31. Police subculture contains many unique elements. What are the two elements that determine the working personality of the police?

A. Threat of danger and authority
B. Isolation and stress
C. Danger and isolation
D. Authority and independence

32. A characteristic of police culture is known as police isolation. This occurs when police officers remove themselves from society because of

    A. programs in which the officer interacts with the public, like the ride along program.

    B. police interaction with society at the worst of times, such as crimes and death.

    C. programs like D.A.R.E.

    D. PALs for community residents.

33. There are various types of stressors that are unique to law enforcement. One type of stress is external stress, which includes

    A. suffering from depression and other health issues.

    B. lack of sleep due to unusual work shifts.

    C. threats of danger that accompany police work.

    D. stress from dealing with the negative aspects of society.

34. Stress that is related to working with negative aspects of a society, which causes distrust in people, is known as

    A. organizational stress.

    B. personal stress.

    C. operational stress.

    D. external stress.

35. Stress that is caused by adjusting your value system in the sub-culture of law enforcement and attempting to get along with your peers is known as

    A. personal stress.

    B. operational stress.

    C. organizational stress.

    D. external stress.

36. In today's modern policing there are new trends that are shaping police departments. These include

    A. DNA analysis for criminal investigations.

    B. body cameras.

    C. the use of technology such as forensics to process crime scenes.

    D. All of the above

37. The term *certiorari* refers to

    A. certification of a court case.
    B. satisfying legal standards.
    C. an order from a higher court asking the lower court for the records for review.
    D. dismissal of a case.

38. Who was the first justice appointed by George Washington?

    A. Franklin Roosevelt
    B. John Jay
    C. William Penn
    D. Thomas Jefferson

39. The United States has a state and federal court system. At the federal level, the courts are divided by district courts that cover federal crimes. How many federal districts are there?

    A. 50
    B. 75
    C. 94
    D. 100

40. The courts that handle felony cases and impose prison sentences are known as

    A. courts of limited jurisdiction.
    B. appeals courts.
    C. courts of general jurisdiction.
    D. family courts.

41. The Court of Appeals is responsible for

    A. imposing sentencing.
    B. determining parole eligibility.
    C. determining probable cause.
    D. reviewing judicial and procedural errors from the lower courts.

42. In the adult court system, the accusatory document that is filed in court is known as a(n)

    A. voucher.
    B. complaint.
    C. indictment.
    D. true bill.

43. In the juvenile court system, the juvenile is referred to as the

A. defendant.
B. delinquent.
C. juvenile offender.
D. minor.

44. In juvenile proceedings, the courts do not use the terms *crimes* or *criminal acts*. They are referred to as

A. delinquent acts.
B. offenses.
C. complaints.
D. charges.

45. In the judicial system, there are many components that make up court proceedings. After the offender has been processed by the police, the next step is

A. booking.
B. grand jury.
C. initial appearance.
D. arraignment.

46. The exchange of information between the prosecutor and the defense, in which the prosecutor relinquishes evidence to the defense to ensure a fair trial, is called

A. discovery.
B. motion.
C. grand jury.
D. information.

47. The United States has a trial process, which is known as

A. inquisitorial.
B. adversarial.
C. democratic.
D. federalist.

48. The United States currently has over 2 million people incarcerated. This number reflects the types of crimes and policies that were prevalent from the 1980s and 1990s; offenses from this specific time frame were predominantly

    A. terrorism and immigration issues.
    B. murders.
    C. identity theft.
    D. drug offenses and "get tough on crime."

49. The Great Law was based on humane Quaker principles and emphasized hard labor in a house of corrections. Who was the founder of the Great Law?

    A. John Jay
    B. George Washington
    C. William Penn
    D. Thomas Jefferson

50. In 1876, Elmira, New York built the first reformatory prison. The reformatory was based on

    A. treatment programs.
    B. treatment for social, biological, and psychological causes of deviant behavior.
    C. adhering to strict work schedules and vocational training.
    D. All of the above

51. Under the correctional system, rehabilitation is

    A. punishing the offender as severely as possible.
    B. punishment that fits the crime, as in "an eye for an eye."
    C. restoring the offender to change his or her future behavior in an effort to return to society positively.
    D. removing the offender from society for as long as possible.

52. Intermediate sanctions

    A. are punishments that are not as severe as prison.
    B. can include monetary fines and sanctions.
    C. include forfeiture of illegal assets and money.
    D. All of the above

53. What is the main goal of the juvenile correctional system?

    A. Rehabilitation
    B. Incarceration
    C. Punishment
    D. Retribution

54. The juvenile justice system is composed of residential treatment programs, which consist of

    A. securing juveniles in jail-like settings.
    B. detox centers for juveniles with drug addiction.
    C. placing juveniles in nonsecured facilities that are monitored by trained members.
    D. community service programs.

55. A probation program that puts a juvenile into a high-risk category and where he or she receives close daily supervision is

    A. parole.
    B. group home confinement.
    C. juvenile probation.
    D. Juvenile Intensive Probation Supervision (JIPS).

56. One of the most famous cases that involved the issue of capital punishment is

    A. *Terry v. Ohio.*
    B. *Furman v. Georgia.*
    C. *Gideon v. Wainwright.*
    D. *Chimel v. California.*

57. Jails are used for multiple purposes, such as

    A. detaining defendants awaiting trial.
    B. detaining defendants that could not make bail.
    C. detaining offenders convicted of misdemeanors.
    D. All of the above

58. The next level of incarceration after jail is

    A. a police booking facility.
    B. prison.
    C. community service.
    D. parole.

59. Prisons are classified into different levels. Medium security consists of

   A. fewer programs for rehabilitation and armed guards and towers.
   B. house arrest.
   C. unsupervised inmate work in locations outside the facility.
   D. a strong emphasis on security, but also education, counseling, and other programs.

60. When an individual is incarcerated, a person may exhibit certain characteristic traits. Prison violence may result and is part of the subculture that is used for many purposes, such as

   A. power.
   B. status.
   C. intimidation.
   D. All of the above

ANSWER KEY AND EXPLANATIONS

1. D	13. C	25. D	37. C	49. C
2. B	14. C	26. C	38. B	50. D
3. D	15. A	27. B	39. C	51. C
4. C	16. D	28. D	40. C	52. D
5. C	17. C	29. A	41. D	53. A
6. D	18. D	30. C	42. B	54. C
7. A	19. D	31. A	43. D	55. D
8. D	20. C	32. B	44. A	56. B
9. C	21. D	33. C	45. C	57. D
10. B	22. B	34. C	46. A	58. B
11. C	23. C	35. A	47. B	59. D
12. D	24. A	36. D	48. D	60. D

1. **The correct answer is D.** Intraracial crime is defined as the victim and offender being from the same race. The majority of crimes are committed between people of the same race. Choices A and B are incorrect because interracial means between different races and biracial concerns people of two races. Choice C is incorrect because statistics indicate that geography and race are key factors in offender/victim relationships.

2. **The correct answer is B.** Mala prohibita are offenses that are prohibited by law and are not wrong in and of themselves. Choice A is incorrect because mala in se offenses, like murder or rape, are considered naturally wrong. Choice C is incorrect because a violation is a prescribed punishment for a low-level offense. Choice D is incorrect because there are no crimes referred to as morality crimes.

3. **The correct answer is D.** Cesare Beccaria believed in the classical criminology theory, in which behavior stems from free will. Choice A is incorrect, as Sigmund Freud was a psychologist and theorized on the subconscious. Choice B is incorrect because Edwin Sutherland believed in a social theory of criminal behavior. Choice C is incorrect because Cesare Lombroso believed in biological determinism.

4. **The correct answer is C.** Freud believed in deviant behavior stemming from psychological and personality disturbances. Choice A is incorrect because the XYY chromosome theory falls under the biological theory. Choice B is incorrect because the labeling theory believes that society creates deviance. Choice D is incorrect because violent crime is a category or type of crime, not an explanation.

5. **The correct answer is C.** Control theory is part of the social process theories, which state that if the bonds of family, church, and school are broken or weakened, this can cause criminality. Choice A is incorrect because classical criminology believes in personal responsibility and free will. Choice B is incorrect because differential association falls under the learning theory. Choice D is incorrect because political crime is a category of crime, not a theory.

6. **The correct answer is D.** Occupational crime is conducted through legal business opportunities. A store clerk who steals merchandise from the store or a cashier who rings up false purchases to steal money are examples. Choice A is incorrect because a felony is defined by punishment of incarceration for more than 366 days. Choice B is incorrect because political crimes are crimes against the state or government. Choice C is incorrect because organized crime deals with acts that are already criminal such as gambling, prostitution, and drugs, and are usually found within enterprises like the mafia.

7. **The correct answer is A.** Visible crime is also known as street crime and includes murder, robbery, and assault. Choice B is incorrect because cybercrime involves the use of computers for illegal activity. Choice C is incorrect because white-collar crime is also known as occupational crime, not street crime. Choice D is incorrect because a misdemeanor is a punishment that can include incarceration for no more than 365 days.

8. **The correct answer is D.** The dark figure of crime is a dimension of crime that occurs but never is reported to the police. Choice A is incorrect because the UCR is the Uniform Crime Report that is generated by the FBI. Choice B is incorrect because "crimes without victims" is a crime category that consists of offenses such as drugs or prostitution and are typically moral issues. Choice C is incorrect because juvenile delinquency involves crimes that are committed by offenders under a certain age.

9. **The correct answer is C.** Juvenile delinquency includes an individual who has committed a crime and is under a certain age. Choice A is incorrect because a neglected child is a child who is receiving inadequate care by their parents. Choice B is incorrect because a dependent child is someone who has no parent or guardian. Choice D is incorrect because a recidivist is someone who is a repeat offender.

10. **The correct answer is B.** Hammurabi was a Babylonian king who established laws to control human behavior and punish offenders through retribution. Choice A is incorrect because Confucius was a Chinese teacher and philosopher. Choice C is incorrect because Caesar was a general and politician for the Roman Republic. Choice D is incorrect because Attila the Hun was the leader of the Hunnic Empire, who wanted to destroy the Roman Empire.

11. **The correct answer is C.** Lex talionis falls under the notion of punishment and retribution. If you break someone's bone they would break your bone. Choice A is incorrect because restitution is the payment by the offender to the victim for any harm that was caused. Choice B is incorrect because it is based on legal fairness and treatment of all individuals. Choice D is incorrect because rehabilitation is the idea of restoring an offender back into society.

12. **The correct answer is D.** Due process guarantees judicial fairness and states that no person shall be deprived of life, liberty, or property, and as such protects all persons in the legal process. Choice A is incorrect because the legislative process takes place when laws are written and passed. Choice B is incorrect because equal protection is found within due process. Choice C is incorrect because the exclusionary rule applies to illegally obtained evidence.

13. **The correct answer is C.** A person cannot be subject to be tried more than once for the same offense in the same jurisdiction by the prosecutor. Choice A is incorrect because the right to be secured in persons and houses falls under the Fourth Amendment. Choice B is incorrect because excessive bail falls under the Eighth Amendment. Choice D is incorrect because the right to legal counsel is in the Sixth Amendment.

14. **The correct answer is C.** The Fruit of the Poisonous Tree Doctrine is under the Fourth Amendment, as it deals with illegal evidence that is obtained during a search. Choice A is incorrect because the Second Amendment primarily deals with the right to bear arms. Choice B is incorrect because the Fifth Amendment is primarily about double jeopardy and self-incrimination. Choice D is incorrect because the Fourteenth Amendment includes the due process clause and fundamental fairness.

15. **The correct answer is A.** The Fourth Amendment protects people from unreasonable searches and seizures, and states that no warrants shall be issued without probable cause. Choice B is incorrect because the Fourteenth Amendment establishes fundamental fairness and the idea that all legal rights are binding to the States. Choice C is incorrect because the Sixth Amendment includes the right to counsel. Choice D is incorrect because the Eighth Amendment prohibits excessive bails, fines, and cruel and unusual punishment.

16. **The correct answer is D.** The Fourteenth Amendment incorporates all the other amendments, including the due process clause, and makes them binding to all the States. Choice A is incorrect because mens rea is not an amendment, but an element of a crime. Choice B is incorrect because protection of self-incrimination is in the Fifth Amendment. Choice C is incorrect because no warrants being issued without probable cause is in the Fourth Amendment.

17. **The correct answer is C.** The exclusionary rule states that any evidence obtained illegally will be excluded from court as inadmissible. Choice A is incorrect because adjudication is the process to determine guilt or innocence. Choice B is incorrect because probable cause is the standard for an arrest. Choice D is incorrect because double jeopardy is subjecting someone to more than one prosecution for the same offense in the same jurisdiction.

18. **The correct answer is D.** Law enforcement is the primary agency within the criminal justice system that maintains public order, keeps the peace, provides social services, enforces the law, and apprehends violators. Choices A, B, and C are incorrect as they have different roles within the criminal justice system.

19. **The correct answer is D.** The correctional system is responsible for the welfare of the defendant and ensures that all sanctions are fulfilled. Corrections operates and manages jails and prisons while also providing rehabilitative services. Choices A and B are incorrect as they have other functions within the criminal justice system. Choice C is also incorrect as family court is limited to hearing cases of juvenile offender status.

20. **The correct answer is C.** Adjudication is the court process that determines if a person is guilty or not guilty. Choice A is incorrect because probable cause is the standard to make an arrest. Choice B is incorrect because beyond a reasonable doubt is the standard for conviction. Choice D is incorrect because a guilty state of mind is mens rea.

21. **The correct answer is D.** The United States works with a dual court system, at both the state level and national or federal level. Choices A, B, and C are all incorrect.

22. **The correct answer is B.** Probation and parole both fall under the correctional system, as probation is part of sentencing and individuals who are paroled are released from prison under strict guidelines and supervision. Choices A, C, and D do not apply to corrections and are incorrect.

23. **The correct answer is C.** The FBI and DEA (Drug Enforcement Agency), are federal agencies, and they are part of the law enforcement system. Choices A and B are incorrect because those agencies are not part of either system. Choice D is incorrect because they may be separate agencies from each other, but both branches are law enforcement agencies.

24. **The correct answer is A.** The death penalty as a prescribed punishment for capital offenses falls under the purview of cruel and unusual punishment, which falls under the Eighth Amendment. Choice B is incorrect because the Fifth Amendment includes double jeopardy and self-incrimination. Choice C is incorrect because the Fourth Amendment deals with unreasonable searches and seizures. Choice D is incorrect because the Sixth Amendment is about the right to counsel and a speedy and public trial.

25. **The correct answer is D.** Policing, along with common law, was based on and founded from English tradition. Therefore, choices A, B, and C are all incorrect as they did not have any influence on American policing or laws.

26. **The correct answer is C.** Peel wanted to reduce conflict by having the police and community work with each other while creating a professional police force. Therefore, choices A, B, and D are all incorrect because they oppose the goals that Robert Peel wanted to accomplish.

27. **The correct answer is B.** The Political Era involved the police and government officials, such as mayors, having close working relationships and providing favors. Choice A is incorrect because community policing stresses a working relationship between the police and the community. Choice C is incorrect because the Professional Era occurred during the Progressive movement and involved getting politics out of policing and establishing a new type of police force. Choice D is incorrect because there is no specific Crime Control Era.

28. **The correct answer is D.** The Progressives were reformers who wanted to remove policing from politics and corruption and establish a well-trained, professional police force. Choices A and B are incorrect because those models do not incorporate these mandates. Choice C is incorrect because there has not been any specific 9/11 era formed as of yet.

29. **The correct answer is A.** The chain of command provides structure, defines ranks within the department including subordinates, and creates accountability and discipline. Choices B, C, and D are all incorrect because none of these terms exists or apply to rank and structure.

30. **The correct answer is C.** D.A.R.E. is a drug prevention program throughout educational and private sectors. Choice A is incorrect because the police may ask for the public's assistance; it does not share investigative techniques. Choice B is incorrect because this is strictly a police officer's role and duty. Choice D is incorrect because this is actually the opposite of what the police do, as they directly get involved in school activities to foster better relationships.

31. **The correct answer is A.** Danger and authority are the two key components that make up the working personality. Choices B, C, and D are all incorrect, as they do not comprise the correct elements of the working personality of the police force.

32. **The correct answer is B.** Police officers often find themselves isolated from the community because of seeing people suffering from death, injuries, and other factors, and includes the tight subculture that is formed. Choices A, C, and D are actually the opposite of police isolation, as these programs are created to help bring the police and the community together.

33. **The correct answer is C.** External stress is often the result of facing threats and dangerous situations, which officers constantly face. Choice A is incorrect because health issues are a result of stress. Choice B is incorrect because lack of sleep due to shift work is organizational stress. Choice D is incorrect because it is the result of operational stress.

34. **The correct answer is C.** Operational stress is the result of distrust of people stemming from dealing with the negative side of society. Choice A is incorrect because organizational stress comes from the inner structure of work. Choice B is incorrect because personal stress occurs when trying to get along with your peers. Choice D is incorrect because external stress comes from the danger of police work.

35. **The correct answer is A.** Personal stress occurs when an individual is adjusting to the law enforcement subculture and reaches a conflict with their value system while trying to get along with their peers. Choices B, C, and D do not fit into this definition and are all incorrect.

36. **The correct answer is D.** Police departments have made large strides in implementing the use of technology, including computers and science, to become more professional and efficient.

37. **The correct answer is C.** Certiorari is a written order for a higher court to review the lower court records. Choices A, B, and D are all incorrect.

38. **The correct answer is B.** John Jay was a Founding Father, who wrote the Federalist Papers, and was the nation's first Chief Justice. Choices A, C, and D are all incorrect.

39. The correct answer is C. There are 94 federal court districts that cover federal crimes. This includes at least one district in each state, as well as the District of Columbia and Puerto Rico. Choices A, B, and D are all incorrect.

40. The correct answer is C. Courts of general jurisdiction hear all felony cases and have the legal authority to sentence individuals to prison. Choice A is incorrect because it hears misdemeanor cases. Choice B is incorrect because the appeals court reviews cases from the lower level courts. Choice D is incorrect because family court hears only family issues and juvenile offender cases.

41. The correct answer is D. Appellate courts do not determine guilt or innocence, but review for any judicial errors from the lower courts. Choice A is incorrect because trial courts impose sentencing. Choice B is incorrect because the parole board determines eligibility. Choice C is incorrect because the courts and prosecutors determine probable cause.

42. The correct answer is B. The accusatory instrument that is filed in adult court is known as the complaint. Choice A is incorrect because a voucher is a police receipt for property. Choice C is incorrect because an indictment is a grand jury proceeding. Choice D is incorrect because a true bill is the document that is produced from a grand jury.

43. The correct answer is D. In the juvenile court system, the juvenile is referred to as the minor. Choice A is incorrect because defendant is for an adult. Choices B and C are incorrect because they refer to juvenile status.

44. The correct answer is A. The criminal acts are referred to as delinquent acts in the juvenile court system. Therefore, choices B, C, and D are all incorrect because the juvenile justice system does not use those terms.

45. **The correct answer is C.** Initial appearance is actually the first step of court proceedings, and occurs when the offender is brought before a judge for the first time to be given their formal notice of charges. Choice A is incorrect because booking is a police procedure and process. Choices B and D are incorrect because they take place later on in the judicial process.

46. **The correct answer is A.** The discovery process is the responsibility of the prosecutor to hand over evidence to the defense that will be introduced in court, so that the defense can prepare its case for a fair trial. Choices B, C, and D are all incorrect because they do not fit into the discovery process.

47. **The correct answer is B.** The adversarial process is one in which both parties argue for their sides as they present their cases and witnesses. Choice A is incorrect because an inquisitorial system is found in Europe, wherein the judge has an active role during the investigation. Choices C and D are both incorrect because they do not fall into the definition of an adversarial system.

48. **The correct answer is D.** Not only were drug offenses soaring during that time, but a new policy of getting tough on crime became the new way of thinking, both culturally and politically. Individuals who are still incarcerated from those times faced stiffer penalties as a result of those policies. Choices A, B, and C are all incorrect, even though they are current issues facing the criminal justice system.

49. **The correct answer is C.** In 1682, William Penn, who was the founder of Pennsylvania, adopted The Great Law. Choices A, B, and D are all incorrect.

50. **The correct answer is D.** The Reformatory Movement began in the 1800s and emphasized treatment of prisoners to determine deviant behavior and rehabilitation.

51. **The correct answer is C.** Rehabilitation is the notion of restoring a person back to society through educational and vocational training. Choices A, B, and D are all incorrect, as they are part of other correctional goals.

52. The correct answer is D. Intermediate sanctions are more restrictive than probation and include all of the methods mentioned, and can work best in combination when they take into account the type of offense that was committed.

53. The correct answer is A. The juvenile justice system is designed for rehabilitation, and one of the main alternatives to incarceration is juvenile probation. Choices B, C, and D are all incorrect as they are not the goals of the juvenile system.

54. The correct answer is C. There are several types of residential treatment programs that are supervised by trained members. Choices A, B, and D are all incorrect as they are not part of any residential programs.

55. The correct answer is D. Juvenile Intensive Probation Supervision (JIPS) is designed as an alternative to incarceration; juveniles are assigned probation officers and receive strict supervision. Choice A is incorrect because parole is for adult prisoners being released from prison. Choice B is incorrect because group home confinement does not fit into juvenile probation. Choice C is incorrect because juvenile probation is for juveniles who are not high risk.

56. The correct answer is B. In *Furman v. Georgia* in 1972, the U.S. Supreme Court banned the use of capital punishment. Choices A, C, and D are all incorrect, as they do not focus on capital punishment issues.

57. The correct answer is D. Jails are facilities that are used for all the reasons mentioned, as well as for holding inmates for federal and state crimes who are awaiting transportation.

58. The correct answer is B. Prisons are the next level of incarceration from jails; they are used for individuals convicted of felony crimes. Choice A is incorrect because police booking facilities are used after an individual is arrested. Choice C is incorrect because community service is a sentence option after a conviction. Choice D is incorrect because parole is an early release from prison.

59. **The court answer is D.** Medium security consists of both armed security and rehabilitative services and programs. Choice A is incorrect because fewer programs and more security is seen at the maximum level. Choice B is incorrect because house arrest consists of a sentence classification in which the defendant is assigned to his or her home under supervision. Choice C is incorrect because this describes minimum security.

60. **The correct answer is D.** Prison violence is a characteristic that is found in prison facilities, and it forms subcultures. Violence is part of the existing subculture, not only inmate on inmate violence but inmate on officer violence as well.

Printed in the USA
CPSIA information can be obtained
at www.ICGtesting.com
JSHW012043140824
68134JS00033B/3240